KNOWING GOOD SCHOOLS

A GUIDE TO RATING PUBLIC HIGH SCHOOLS

DOROTHY WARNER AND
WILLIAM D. GUTHRIE

BERGIN & GARVEY
WESTPORT, CONNECTICUT • LONDON

Library of Congress Cataloging-in-Publication Data

Warner, Dorothy, 1948–
    Knowing good schools : a guide to rating public high schools / Dorothy Warner and
William D. Guthrie.
      p. cm.
    Includes bibliographical references and index.
    ISBN 0–89789–739–0 (alk. paper)
      1. School choice—United States—Handbooks, manuals, etc. 2. High schools—
United States—Evaluation—Handbooks, manuals, etc. 3. High schools—United
States—Case studies. I. Guthrie, William D., 1935– II. Title.
    LB1027.9.W37 2001
    373.73—dc21   00–048604

British Library Cataloguing in Publication Data is available.

Library of Congress Catalog Card Number: 00–048604
ISBN: 0–89789–739–0

First published in 2001

Bergin & Garvey, 88 Post Road West, Westport, CT 06881
An imprint of Greenwood Publishing Group, Inc.
www.greenwood.com

Printed in the United States of America

The paper used in this book complies with the
Permanent Paper Standard issued by the National
Information Standards Organization (Z39.48–1984).

10 9 8 7 6 5 4 3 2 1

Dedicated to Rhoda Garoogian, in memory

Contents

Acknowledgments

Rhoda Garoogian first introduced the idea of a book about effective schools to us and we are grateful for the challenge that she presented. The following individuals were both supportive and encouraging of the need for this endeavor and gave willingly of their time. We are grateful to the staff of Delaware Valley Regional High School, especially Martin J. Matula, Michael J. Billas, James Kasenga, and Linda Kreuzweiser; to the staff of Council Rock High School, especially F. David Yates and Teresa Androutsos; to the staff of Bayonne High School, especially Michael A. Wanko, Joan Rosen, and Georgiann Gongora. These individuals confirmed our pride of public schools and of those who work so very hard at making our school system an exemplary one. Special thanks to Karl Merzena for his technical assistance. Rider University awarded a Summer Fellowship in support of the research for this project and that gift of time was invaluable. To John Buschman, Joshua David Karlowich, and Evelyn Guthrie—thank you for believing in us.

Introduction

A friend and educator invited us to write a book about "best schools" in the United States and thus began our journey into just what it means to be "best." We realized that what is "best" for one student is not necessarily "best" for another. We were also concerned that frequently the measure of a school is solely its performance on achievement tests, without consideration of other processes taking place within the school. Schools have more comprehensive missions than high achievement scores. We quickly realized that because of our backgrounds in education we are at an advantage in assessing schools and we recognized that there is a need for a clear assessment tool to be used by both nonprofessionals and professionals alike. We had to ask ourselves, exactly, "How *do* we *know* a good school?"

From the beginning we knew that we wanted to celebrate the public school system in the United States. From our experience, public schools take their responsibility of serving every citizen very seriously and the schools have ambitious educational goals. The right that each of us has to be educated is one that many of us take for granted, failing to see the lifelong opportunity that we are given by that education.

With our research into effective education literature we were reminded of the constant evaluation and assessment process within good schools and the willingness of public schools to embrace educational ideas and opportunities. A good school is always "in process." We have tried to provide a glimpse into that process as well as bring some understanding to its results.

In reviewing the final manuscript we are aware of an area of assessment that is yet to be clearly developed. Schools assess academic achievement in multiple ways. Yet public schools are also preparing students to be contributing citizens in a complex community. How can we adequately assess this area and what it actually means to be "prepared," including the "internalization of societal values" (Bobbitt, Quinn, & Dabbs, 1992, p. 2)? We encourage schools to continue to explore this important aspect of assessment.

Our focus on high schools was intentional. The high school is the "proof of the pudding" in the school district. If one is considering a school district, whether or not the student is high school age, it is wise to consider the high school as well as the "feeding schools." The curriculum will be coordinated with all levels of schooling in the district and the future schooling of a child is equally as important as the earlier years.

We have directed the book toward a primary audience of parents seeking a good high school for their children. Educators interested in school assessment will find this a useful tool as well. By educators we are considering teacher educators, school administrators, teachers, and those who choose alternative education routes. We also hope that the book will serve as a guide for citizens who wish to inform themselves about their public schools. It is our hope that this book will foster an understanding of, and a sense of knowing about, the purposes of schools. Well-informed citizens can best help their schools and promote education's position within our society. We were welcomed into schools to evaluate the schools' effectiveness and each time our own understanding of schools grew. We invite you to get to know your own schools better.

CHAPTER 1

What Makes a Good American High School?

UNCOVERING PURPOSES AND GOALS OF HIGH SCHOOLS

To define the fundamental purposes of any public high school in the United States it is necessary first to reflect on the nature of our country. It is a changing, developing nation that initially consciously sought to be different from the Europe that so many of its early colonial inhabitants came from. It has since tried to develop ways to be thoroughly democratic and free. Many current purposes and practices stem from roots that have grown over the years. It is only natural, then, that our exploration into the assessment of high schools will begin with a review of the historical underpinnings of secondary education in the United States. We will seek to identify the stated purposes of high schools as they have emerged over the years and trace significant changes that have occurred in educational theory and practice. Any useful assessment of a high school must be based on its stated purposes and goals in the context of the history of secondary education in the United States.

CHARACTERISTICS OF EDUCATION IN THE UNITED STATES

The correct answer to the question, "What is the American national educational system like?" is, "There is no national American educational system." The U.S. Constitution does not address education, deferring to "states' rights." All states have constitutions that clearly indicate that the individual state has full jurisdiction for education. So, there are fifty education systems that constitute education in the United States. The federal government's role over the years has been one of making persuasive recommendations to states, providing financial aid for particular efforts, encouraging and supporting educational research, and passing legislation affecting schools such as civil rights legislation. It has no direct jurisdiction over public schools.

Despite the very real fact that there is no national educational system, there are basic characteristics of education in the United States that have made it quite unique in the world. From the beginning of this modern nation, leaders expressed fundamental ideas on which states have enacted educational policies and practices. In a letter written in 1786 to George Washington, Thomas Jefferson directly linked instruction (schooling) to the maintenance of liberty by saying that liberty can never be safe unless it is in the hands of the people who have instruction. He added that it was the business of the states to plan for such instruction, thus clearly outlining the basic notion that the states must provide public education to make sure liberty is maintained (Boyd, 1950). By proposing to the Virginia legislature that local citizens provide publicly supported elementary schools to prepare children for citizenship, he stressed that these schools would be a public investment in the preparation of people capable of self-government and individual growth. Schools, then, would provide for personal educational development leading to societal development and an orderly government.

In the New England colonies the Massachusetts Act of 1647 mandated that all towns of fifty or more families must establish reading schools and towns of one hundred or more families must establish grammar schools. In this earlier development, the stated purposes of schooling were to enable citizens to read and understand the Bible but, in many cases, also to become better citizens (Button & Provenzo, 1983).

Pennsylvania, like Massachusetts, took on the mission of educating youth before Jefferson proclaimed the idea that individual states should have such a mission. Benjamin Franklin, for example, had earlier proposed a plan for the education of youth in Pennsylvania in which he stressed the idea that schools should provide useful (practical) studies: ones that stressed service and opportunities to pursue occupational interests. The obvious difference in the way these two states approached schooling indicates just how different states would continue to be different in the way they conceptualized and practiced education.

Benjamin Rush, a signer of the Declaration of Independence and professor at the University of Pennsylvania, in the late eighteenth century proposed that Pennsylvania develop a comprehensive system of public education (i.e., provide schools and colleges for all levels of education). His idea was that the new nation must educate its own citizens (and leaders) rather than have them be forced to be educated in foreign lands that might not embrace democratic values and ideals. He, along with Noah Webster, stressed that our own nation must offer education essential to the maintenance of a free society and government and that an educated citizenry and educated leaders were essential for the development and maintenance of an orderly society. This early idea of a comprehensive system of public education was to grow into a distinctive characteristic of American education.

In the days of the formation of this nation, many ideas circulated as people sought to create a nation quite different from those found in Europe. This new nation would provide, among other things, common education ensuring that all would have the chance to succeed. But the likelihood of moving quickly to such radically different schooling seemed remote in the eighteenth century. The schooling that had been familiar to people coming to America from Europe was one that very much depended on the social and economic standing of parents. So, in early America as in Europe, educational opportunities were extended mainly to males, and public funds for education went to colleges and academies (primarily serving the rich) or schools for the poor. The vast middle stratum of society was neglected. The idea of educating the whole citizenry, however, was apparently in the minds of our forefathers as they considered the implications of creating a democracy in which there would be opportunities for all to succeed in their individual pursuits.

EMERGENCE OF THE COMMON SCHOOL

It was out of the experiences of towns, primarily in New England, that were publicly supporting schools that the "Common School" emerged. Common schools were schools supported by taxes and therefore no fees were charged for attendance and so they were free. These schools were also open to all children regardless of family disposition and so they were universal. Although these common schools were neighborhood oriented, as the population grew they also expanded to include more than just one neighborhood.

Horace Mann, secretary of the Massachusetts State Board of Education in the mid-nineteenth century, became the most recognized major advocate of the common school. He believed that education would be a practical and effective way to deal with the social problems related to industrialization affecting Massachusetts at that time. As rural workers flocked to the cities for work, their living and working conditions became deplorable. In contrast to the relatively homogenous small-town atmosphere from which they came, workers found a strange workplace filled with people having different backgrounds and beliefs and one in which they were treated more as "cogs in a wheel" than respected as individuals with personal dignity. In the midst of this turmoil, Horace Mann believed that the nature of the common school provided the appropriate institution to help solve many problems. Its nonsectarian orientation would help accommodate the wide range of differing morals and beliefs of the families by teaching universal principles rather than the narrow views normally encountered in homogenous small-town societies. Its expandable structure would handle the increased number of students that was producing a high population density. It was believed that the common school would assimilate students by developing skills with which to live in a complex society, including inculcating a Protestantlike work ethic. Common schools were designed to serve all the students in a region and so various aspects of such schooling should have supported this idea. Two aspects are especially important: (1) providing instruction that would be personalized, and (2) providing the opportunity for schooling for all socioeconomic levels (Urban & Wagoner, 2000).

To ensure appropriate instruction, Horace Mann promoted a type of teaching based on the ideas of Johann Heinrich Pestalozzi, a Swiss educator. This way of teaching is to begin by attracting the attention of students with an actual object and then studies would follow the interests of students. Such a strategy would clearly support the ideals of democracy, especially the development of free individuals, but it flew in the face of the way lessons were normally taught. Traditional teaching was basically lecture followed by recitation. Lecturing ensured the study of approved views and effected maximum control of content and behavior. So, even though Pestalozzi's instructional model closely matched democratic ideals, the common schools largely maintained the traditional instructional strategies despite educational theorists like Horace Mann espousing ideas like those of Pestalozzi. The school in New Harmony, Indiana, did, however, develop a full and systematic application of Pestalozzi's theories and school practice. By its very structure, however, the common school brought together students of diverse backgrounds and abilities and represented a major step toward achieving the ideals of our forefathers: educating the whole citizenry.

Stating purposes of education and the related means to accomplish them became increasingly important in the later nineteenth century. In these years as the common school movement blossomed into the development of school systems, an extension of the idea that schools would serve societal purposes developed: compulsory school attendance. By the early twentieth century all states had adopted compulsory school attendance laws. Child labor was later regulated with laws, but initially state governments used mandatory school attendance to keep children out of the labor market. The inclusion of students of diverse backgrounds into one school and compulsory school attendance produced an immediate increase in the proportion of children in schools.

DEVELOPMENT OF PUBLIC HIGH SCHOOLS

In colonial America the first attempt to provide schooling beyond the elementary school was the Latin grammar school. This secondary school was established to offer preparation for college and provide for general education. The purpose of the schools was for the colonial elite to establish or maintain their place in society and, because knowledge of Greek and Latin was the mark of an educated or well-bred man, the nature of the school matched its purpose.

Students enrolled in Latin grammar schools were from the most influential and affluent families. The curriculum was based on the classics typically studied in European Latin schools and teachers were usually men who were ministers not serving a particular church at the time. It was in this context that Benjamin Franklin proposed a new kind of secondary school. His academy would educate all worthy students regardless of social class and have a program of studies that would produce trained workers who would become effective participants in the new national economy. Although Franklin's academy did not require the study of Latin and Greek, the classics were taught along with subjects such as arithmetic, accounting, astronomy, geometry, navigation, English, modern languages, gardening, and good breeding. Because most students paid fees and admittance required previously learned reading and writing skills, poor boys were essentially excluded. Excluded also were all girls and persons of color (George et al., 2000, pp. 3–4).

In the period from 1781 to 1825 academies, which were normally chartered by states as legal entities under the control of boards of trustees, were the most rapidly multiplying schools in the United States. These schools were normally college preparatory or sometimes served as alternatives to college. They inevitably replaced the Latin Grammar School and many existing entrepreneurial or private venture schools. Academies were established throughout the nation. The curriculum of the academy often continued study of classical subjects, reflecting the earlier Latin grammar schools, but went beyond that (Button & Provenzo, 1983).

Academies, controlled by independent boards or churches, were gradually replaced with high schools. High schools are secondary schools supported by taxes and controlled by public authorities. The name high school may have come from the Edinburgh High School founded much earlier and funded by the city of Edinburgh, Scotland, that had been visited by a prominent Bostonian. The term was used to name the English High School in Boston, originally established as the Boston English Classical School in 1821. This school is generally regarded as the first free public high school in the United States (Button & Provenzo, 1983).

Building on the "common school" idea, which basically was supposed to instill in elementary school children the moral and civil basis for society, during the late nineteenth century public (tax-supported) high schools were developed first in urban areas and then more extensively. Even though Massachusetts, in 1827, adopted a law requiring towns of more than 4,000 people to establish free public high schools, the high school movement spread slowly across the nation. By the time of the Civil War there were only about 300 high schools in America, twenty-six of them in Massachusetts (Pulliam & Van Patten, 1995).

Common elementary schools and a state university were developed in Michigan, but students going to college needed to attend a private secondary school. Most students except those who could afford private secondary education stopped their education after the elementary school. When public high schools were proposed to fill in the gap between elementary schools and colleges, a citizen in Kalamazoo challenged the proposal. The Michigan state supreme court, responding to the challenge, determined that the Michigan legislature had, in fact, already developed a system for schooling, elementary through university, and that the high school would be a logical part of that system. This landmark decision became the rationale for establishing public high schools in other states (Urban & Wagoner, 2000).

High school programs of study across the nation changed from a common curriculum (as in the common school), to ones providing a choice of studies to students. But the development of high schools across the various states also instituted another significant characteristic of American schooling: publicly supported educational opportunity for all through high school. Not all states, however, instituted public support for education beyond high school through to the college/university level. If all children were to be given the opportunity for high school education, it followed logically that the high school curriculum must provide for a range of diverse interests.

The "Committee of Ten," a committee of the National Education Association, issued a report in 1894 recommending four different program offerings that students were to be able to choose from in a high school: Classical, Latin-Scientific, Modern Languages, or English (National Education Association, 1894). It was thought that any one of these programs would prepare students for life beyond high school, whether in the workplace, college, or the home. These four programs were thought to greatly promote social mobility. Like the earlier ideas formulated by influential individuals, committees of national educational organizations developed and issued reports that were designed to influence states to enact, either through administrative or legislative action, new ways of educating youth. In many states, individual high schools could take action on their own, and many did so.

THE RISE OF VOCATIONAL EDUCATION

Soon pressure mounted to include training programs in the high school that were linked to commerce and industry. The Smith-Hughes Act of 1917 provided national support for vocational education. Many high schools adopted curriculum differentiation (tracking) in terms of commercial, vocational, and academic programs. It soon became clear, however, that there was an obvious correlation between social classes and curriculum programs. This sensed connection was later clearly delineated in the 1933 U.S. Bureau of Education Bulletin, *The Program of Studies*, part of the report of the National Survey of Secondary Education (Loomis, 1933). The study showed a direct relationship between socioeconomic level and measured intelligence level and between socioeconomic level and curriculum type (e.g., Academic versus Household Arts or Industrial Arts programs). This relationship contradicted the idea of equal educational opportunity, but was tolerated as high schools were becoming focused more on economic goals than other social and civic ones. The need for vocational education in American schooling has been recognized throughout its history. Just how to provide for it has been a continuing question. As you will see, three alternatives to solving this dilemma will emerge. One solution is to have a specialized vocational high school in which students attend part-time and spend the other part in a comprehensive "home" high school. A second solution is to have vocational courses offered as part of the curriculum of a comprehensive high school. A third solution is not to have any designated vocational courses, but to have a high school program that prepares students for any future including both college and work—that is, high school as an academic institution.

PROGRESSIVE EDUCATION: THE EIGHT-YEAR STUDY

Embedded in a period in American history called the Progressive Era, occurring in the early twentieth century, is the progressive education movement. Growing from the increase of social conscience and changes in culture, the larger progressive reforms, beginning in the late 1880s were designed to improve government, assist the exploited, and increase general efficiency (Button & Provenzo, 1983). In the 1920s the educational dimension of the progressive movement had individuality and freedom as its most common themes. Perhaps the movement was a protest against traditional teaching and the application of doctrines of social efficiency and control (Krug, 1964).

One of the most significant long-term experiments involving American high schools took place during the Progressive Era and was called the Eight-Year Study. It is important because it sets the stage for our modern school systems. The Progressive Education Association established the Commission on the Relation of School and College in 1930. This commission conducted an experimental study involving three hundred accredited colleges and universities across the United States, including highly regarded Harvard, Yale, and the like. These colleges agreed to accept graduates of thirty high schools, beginning in 1936, whose educators were given complete autonomy to develop teaching and learning activities and curriculum based on theories of the Progressive Education Association. That is, all the traditional college entrance requirements were waived and the schools were free to implement, in their own fashion, what would be related to the association's seven-point platform. That platform included the following: (1) there should be freedom of students to develop naturally; (2) interest, the motive of all work, should be a central consideration in curriculum and instruction; (3) the teacher should be a guide, not a taskmaster; (4) teachers should engage in the scientific study of pupil development and use the results in their instructional practices; (5) the school should give attention to all that affects the child's physical development; (6)

there should be cooperation between home and school; and (7) the progressive school should be a leader in educational movements (Progressive Education Association, 1938).

After studying the results of the experiment known as the Eight-Year Study that was prepared under the direction of Ralph Tyler, head of the Bureau of Educational Research at Ohio State University, the Commission on the Relation of School and College prepared a three-volume report detailing their conclusions. Wilford M. Aiken, in the first volume, *The Story of the Eight-Year Study*, summarized the study's findings with three general conclusions and five specific ones about the high school curriculum. "First, the assumption that preparation for the liberal arts college depends upon the study of certain prescribed subjects in the secondary school is no longer tenable." The commission found that various quite different high school programs in schools involved in the experiment each led to college success. "The second major implication of the results of the Eight-Year Study is that secondary schools can be trusted with a greater measure of freedom than college requirements now permit." As a result of the effective programs developed by the schools in the experiment, the commission called for colleges and high schools to work cooperatively to ascertain the essential knowledge, skills, habits, and qualities of mind and character needed for college preparation. The third major conclusion concerned the central purpose of the school, recognizing that it must be related to the purposes of the society that maintains the schools. "It follows, therefore, that the chief purpose of education in the United States should be to preserve, promote, and refine the way of life (democratic living) in which we as a people believe" (Aiken, 1942, pp. 118, 124, 132). With respect to the high school curriculum, the commission came to these conclusions:

First, every student should achieve competence in the essential skills of communication—reading, writing, oral expression—and in the use of quantitative concepts and symbols.

Second, inert subject matter should give way to content that is alive and pertinent to the problems of youth and modern civilization.

Third, the common, recurring concerns of American youth should give content and form to the curriculum.

Fourth, the life and work of the school should contribute, in every possible way, to the physical, mental and emotional health of every student.

Fifth, the curriculum in its every part should have one clear, major purpose. That purpose is to bring every young American his great heritage of freedom, to develop understanding of the kind of life we seek, and to inspire devotion to human welfare. (Aiken, 1942, p. 138)

Although the progressive education movement was not to last, the Eight-Year Study remains an excellent model of educational experimentation and its findings still inform current reforms. Linda Darling-Hammond's description of the study captures some of its salient points.

Like the highly successful schools of today's reform initiatives, these school communities were small and organized around internally developed goals. They sought to build a core curriculum linked to community concerns as well as to students' interests and developmental needs. The schools that showed the most extraordinary successes were those that differed most from mainstream practice: their teaching was the most experimental and inquiry oriented and their governance systems the most democratic. (Darling-Hammond, 1997, p. 10)

THE COMPREHENSIVE HIGH SCHOOL

The device to bring the high school back to a semblance of common schooling was the "Comprehensive High School." The comprehensive high school is an American creation, foreign to educators in other countries, according to James Conant (in 1967). He saw it as a product of our history. As free high schools developed in communities under the authority of states it became accepted doctrine that education should be provided for all youth regardless of their ambitions and abilities. Instead of being selective, like their European counterparts, American high schools became elective. All students elected courses from a number of offerings, with some of the curriculum devoted to a set of required courses. Because all students entered the school regardless of their educational aims, and compulsory attendance laws increased attendance, the schools became more heterogeneous. This bringing together of students having different backgrounds was considered an advantage of the public school. Youth from a variety of backgrounds would come to understand each other. The justification of the comprehensive high school is often stated in terms of social and political ideals. It seeks to develop the basis of a common democratic understanding while through its elective offerings provide excellent academic preparation and rewarding vocational education (Conant, 1967).

In 1915, the National Education Association appointed a commission named the Commission on the Reorganization of Secondary Education, later commonly referred to as the Committee of Ten. Clarence Kingsley, a mathematics teacher who had recently become inspector of high schools in Massachusetts, was chairman of the commission. In a 1918 report, "Cardinal Principles of Secondary Education," the following seven principal objectives of the high school were proposed: health, command of fundamental processes, worthy home membership, vocation, citizenship, worthy use of leisure, and ethical character. In a follow-up study by the National Education Association's Department of Superintendence in 1928, it was reported that respondents to a questionnaire to high school principals across the country took action on reorganizing their schools. Essentially they added subjects such as commercial studies, social studies, industrial arts, physical and biological sciences, and home economics, and dropped Latin, ancient history, French, and advanced mathematics. The seven principles were adopted by others such as the National Congress of Parents and Teachers, and have been discussed by educators throughout the years since its release (Krug, 1964). Clearly, this report provided a rationale for the idea of a comprehensive high school in which all children up to age eighteen would be in the same school but have curriculum choices across a range of subjects and experiences spanning academic ones (in preparation for college) to industrial ones (in preparation for work).

Along with the development of the comprehensive high school came the development of cocurricular programs to provide common activities for students otherwise engaged in various separate subjects of choice that would segregate students. These activities would mix students together regardless of their academic or preparation for work programs. The Committee of Ten report called for the high school to provide for common student activities like athletics, social events, and school government. High schools had been providing such activities for years, but now they would have the identified purpose of unifying the student body (Krug, 1964). Some educators make a distinction between cocurricular and extracurricular activities to distinguish the relationship of such student activities to the school's curriculum. Although considered interchangeable terms in the later guidelines developed to help you evaluate a high school, the use of one or the other of the terms is an indication of the purpose for offering them in a particular high school.

CREATING UNIFORMITY IN SCHOOL PROGRAMS

As high school offerings became differentiated, the need arose to have objective ways to determine which students were suited for the various programs. So, more extensive objective tests and systematic testing programs began to be developed. The College Entrance Examination Board, created in 1900, produced uniform college entrance examinations and, in effect, created considerable national uniformity in high school academic programs. Simultaneously, the Carnegie Foundation proposed a way to standardize credit for high school work based on time—specifically the number of required hours of classroom instruction. The "Carnegie Unit" became the normal way of measuring high school course credit. One unit is defined as 120 hours of instruction (class sessions being 40 to 60 minutes in length, meeting four to five times per week, for 36 to 40 weeks a year).

To further establish common standards for high schools, the Commission on Accredited Schools was created in 1901 and the first of what would become six regional accreditation associations was initiated. These regional accreditation associations, still in existence, engage schools in self-study. The schools are then visited by teams of educators selected by the association from outside the school system. Each team develops a report based on their reactions to the school's self-study and their observations and interviews conducted on the visit to the school. In the report, the team makes recommendations to the school and delivers a report to the regional association having jurisdiction over the region in which the school is located. By being "accredited," high schools ensure that graduates will gain admission to colleges. Normally a student must graduate from a regionally accredited high school and have a particular level of achievement on the Scholastic Aptitude Test (SAT) or the American College Testing Program (ACT) to be admitted to a college or university that is also accredited by one of the regional associations.

CALLS FOR HIGHER ACADEMIC STANDARDS AND NATIONAL GOALS

Criticisms of schools over the last two or three decades are not something new. American education has experienced criticism over its whole existence and has a long tradition of innovation as well. But the kinds of criticisms have differed over the years. Early attacks on the colonial schools for being only for the elite have continued in the tradition of assuring free education for all. As immigrants streamed into the United States, education was to provide shared values to assure a "melting pot." Offering vocational education was a priority as urbanization and industrialization became significant. As social progressivism grew to supply the needs of citizens, progressives attacked traditional educational practices. With the Great Depression and World War II came a repudiation of everything progressive and pleas for a return to traditional discipline and the centrality of subject knowledge. One of these early calls for reform was in the form of a book published in 1953 by Arthur Bestor, *Educational Wastelands: The Retreat from Learning in Our Public Schools*. Bestor blasted progressive education as being actually regressive in nature and urged that disciplined intelligence must be reestablished. He believed that the integrated curriculum and vocationalism were not productive (George et al., 2000).

When the Russians embarrassed Americans in the space race by putting Sputnik in orbit around the earth, there was a responsive cry that the U.S. education system was at fault because of a lack of emphasis on scientific studies. Soon, the National Defense Education Act was legislated to make available financial support for science, mathematics, social studies, foreign language, and guidance programs in schools. This identification of special programs to be supported by the federal government was a harbinger of the use of financial incentives to encourage desired educational developments in schools. The federal financial support, of course, promotes the ideas held by the federal administration and Congress at the time of the initiation of the support program.

A far-reaching decision of the U.S. Supreme Court in 1954 established that racially segregated schools deprived individuals of equal protection of the laws. In the case, *Brown et al. versus Board of Education of Topeka et al.*, the court decided that education was probably the most important function of state and local governments and that it was the foundation of citizenship. The court went on to say that schooling was the principal way to awaken children to cultural values, prepare them for later professional training, and help them adjust to the environment. Therefore, educational opportunity must be provided to everyone on equal terms. The doctrine of separate but equal has no place in American education. This, and subsequent state court decisions, led to a variety of desegregation efforts in schools, including transporting students across neighborhoods to other schools and thereby eliminating or reducing segregation of races but, at the same time, altering the traditional neighborhood school concept. The civil rights movement of the 1960s led to further changes promoting equal educational opportunity, including affirmative action policies.

As an example of the cycles of educational criticism and reform in America, Nelson, Palonsky, and Carlson point out that during the 1950s the criticisms directed at progressive education were attended by the promotion of scholarly rigor, academic excellence, and avoidance of mediocrity. In reacting to what was considered conservative authoritarianism and dehumanization of schools, reforms of the 1960s like open education, more student freedom, abolition of dress codes, relaxation of rigid rules of conduct, and initiation of new course electives were common (Nelson et al., 2000).

Curriculum reforms in the 1960s exerted much influence in schools. National curriculum development projects were formed involving the nation's most prominent scholars and curriculum theorists. Many of these study groups adopted teaching strategies known as inquiry or discovery that were much more learner centered and activity oriented than traditional strategies, and materials were written to support these new strategies. In 1954 the National Science Foundation, an agency of the federal government, began to fund summer institutes for science teachers, then two years later science teaching films; it then produced a radically new physics course of study known as PSSC Physics (Physical Science Study Committee). Other courses of study followed, such as the Biological Sciences Curriculum Study (BSCS) that involved three approaches to high school biology (green—ecological, blue—biochemical, and yellow—taxonomic), and the School Mathematics Study Group (SMSG) mathematics program. These courses reflected significant changes in both content and teaching strategies. This top-down curriculum reform worked best in schools in which teachers acted as partners in translating and incorporating ideas that were at the base of these projects into their school programs. When teachers were expected to adopt and implement programs whose development they felt no part of, the programs died (Darling-Hammond, 1997). New math (SMSG), for example, was considered by many students and parents to be a mysterious and nonpractical program while others thought it was a wonderful innovation.

Free and appropriate educational opportunity for all children is an idea that has evolved since colonial times in America. In 1974 the U.S. Congress passed a law that demonstrated that the concept clearly applied to handicapped children. Public Law 94–142, the Education of All Children Act, put into practice what is known as mainstreaming. According to this law, students with special needs who demonstrate appropriate behavior and skills should be included in regular classrooms rather than placed in separate ones away from regular students. Another aspect of the law required that schools have facilities for handicapped students that provided the least restrictive environment. The law was intended to assure that students with special needs would have all the advantages of schooling available to other students. Such federal legislation has affected most public high schools because it applies to all institutions that use federal funds.

In 1990 modifications were made to Public Law 94–142 that extended the idea of mainstreaming to expectation of inclusion. The Individuals with Disabilities Education Act (IDEA), which is the updated Education for All Children Act, requires schools to educate students with disabilities with other students to the maximum extent possible. Notice the change in language from "handicapped" to "disabled" in the 1990 modification. Schools must provide supplementary aids and services for disabled students and these children cannot be removed from regular classrooms unless they cannot learn in the regular setting even with supplementary aids and services. The modifications have improved the educational rights of children from being mainstreamed to full inclusion (Turnbull & Turnbull, 1998).

Just how high schools respond to these laws depends on how they see their educational goals and how they can organize and teach while taking into consideration the variety of differences in learners. There are many possibilities and it is interesting to observe just how a particular school is responding to these challenges. Just as schools were considering how to respond to Public Law 94–142, a series of national reports were issued calling for more attention to academic excellence. This became another step in the cycles of educational criticisms and reforms.

A report of the National Commission on Excellence in Education issued by the U.S. Department of Education in 1983, *A Nation at Risk*, recommended higher academic and student conduct standards for high schools. The report criticized schools for being mediocre and recommended that they emphasize five "basics": four years of English, three years of mathematics, three years of science, three years of social studies, and one half-year of computer science. This report, widely reported in the media, resulted in a reexamination of standards and procedures in high schools. *A Nation at Risk* spawned many other reports from individuals and groups. The general thrust of these other reports blasted the plethora of special courses designed for student interests and favored having a substantial core of academic courses for all (harking back to one of the ideas of the common school) and emphasizing the need for strict academic standards.

Mortimer Adler's "The Paideia Proposal" was a generally conservative report expressing the need for academic rigor and the development of intellectual skills in American schools in 1982. His proposal became the base of the National Paideia Center at the University of North Carolina at Greensboro that currently works to encourage and support the systematic reform of American public schools based on the principles in the Paideia Proposal. At present there are over 100 schools in twelve states that have become committed to the

Paideia principles and associated with the National Paideia Center. The principles stated by the Paideia Council include the following ideas. All children can learn and deserve the same quality of schooling and the best education for the best is the best education for all. Schooling should be preparation for becoming generally educated throughout the course of a lifetime and should prepare all Americans to earn a decent livelihood, be good citizens, and make a good life for themselves. Genuine learning is primarily the activity of the learner's own mind, sometimes with the help of a teacher. Teachers should use didactic (expository or lecture) teaching, coaching skills of learning, and Socratic questioning in seminars so that students will acquire organized knowledge, form habits of skills in the use of language and mathematics, and grow in the mind's understanding of basic ideas and issues. Student achievement should be evaluated in terms of competencies and not solely compared to the achievements of others. The principal should be a leading teacher cooperatively engaged with teachers in planning, reforming, and reorganizing the school as an educational community and, along with the teachers, actively engaged in learning. Continuing to learn should be the prime motivation of professional educators.

Adler's proposal is considered one of the more conservative reports developed in the early 1980s. Other conservative reports include the Twentieth-Century Fund's *Making the Grade* (1983), the College Entrance Examination Board's *Academic Preparation for College* (1983), and the National Science Foundation's *Educating Americans for the 21st Century* (1983). More liberal reports include John Goodlad's *A Place Called School* (1984) and Theodore Sizer's *Horace's Compromise* (1984). Ernest Boyer's *High School* (1983) is considered a more moderate report (Nelson et al., 2000).

In retrospect, it seems that American schools were actually much better than the U.S. government reports and media stories described during the 1980s. Findings given in the *Sandia Report* submitted to the Department of Energy in 1992, a thorough study of American education produced by the Sandia National Laboratories, showed that U.S. schools were doing quite well and that government educational policy was being based on misinterpretations of data. The *Sandia Report* noted that their research simply did not support claims that there was a systemwide failure in education. There is evidence that the government subjected the report to delays and revisions, which caused a two-year lag in being released to the public and was effective in suppressing the impact of the information (Nelson et al., 2000, pp. 8–9).

National Education Goals

In March 1994 the U.S. Congress enacted legislation with the stated purpose of establishing national education goals. Of the seven goals given in the law, several specifically addressed high schools:

School Completion. By the year 2000, the high school graduation rate will increase to at least 90 percent.

Student Achievement and Citizenship. By the year 2000, all students will leave grades 4, 8, and 12 having demonstrated competency over challenging subject matter including English, mathematics, science, foreign languages, civics and government, economics, arts, history, and geography, and every school in America will ensure that all students learn to use their minds well, so they may be prepared for responsible citizenship, further learning, and productive employment in our Nation's modern economy.

Mathematics and Science. By the year 2000, United States students will be first in the world in mathematics and science achievement.

Safe, Disciplined, and Alcohol- and Drug-free Schools. By the year 2000, every school in the United States will be free of drugs, violence, and the unauthorized presence of firearms and alcohol and will offer a disciplined environment conducive to learning.

Parental Participation. By the year 2000, every school will promote partnerships that will increase parental involvement and participation in promoting social, emotional, and academic growth of children (Public Law 103–227).

These goals, of course, are only offered to states for their consideration and possible adoption. They were legislated at the national level and no action could be taken unless states and local school districts agreed, since the national government does not have jurisdiction over education. Responding to the offer of grants, however, forty-nine states have received funds to develop state standards-based educational improvements, acknowledging participation in the federal Goals 2000.

During the 1990s there were a number of studies and reports describing high schools and making recommendations for reform. For example, a report of the National Association of Secondary School Principals in partnership with the Carnegie Foundation for the Advancement of Teaching, titled *Breaking Ranks: Changing an Institution*, was published in 1996. The report is an attempt to focus on high school goals and call on schools to become more personalized, have higher expectations for student performance, and demonstrate a sense of purpose. Nine major purposes of the high school form the basis for their specific recommendations. This report, along with other significant reports, is considered in more detail later in this chapter.

Over the years to the present, public high schools in the United States have engaged in identifying missions and purposes. These missions and purposes have evolved as society, academic knowledge, and technology have evolved. In the current statements of high school purposes and missions, one can recognize the present conditions, concerns, and aspirations of the citizens as well as reflections of the deeper roots representing ideals that stretch back to those of this nation's founders.

ALTERNATIVES TO PUBLIC SCHOOLING

Throughout the history of the United States parents have had the freedom to choose whether their children would attend public schools or be engaged in education in some other form. Schooling of some sort, however, is mandated by states. School choice is a current issue that has many facets. Traditionally, across the United States students attend schools in their own neighborhood or district. The school district normally is aligned with a government designation (e.g., a city or township, etc.). With the advent of regional school districts, several school districts join to form a larger district, thereby crossing over government lines. These more extensive school districts involve transporting students as well as managing relations between the various communities involved. As school districts grow and develop several schools, the matter of choice of school within a given district emerges. For the most part, these matters have been subject to strict rules regarding local districting within the larger district. Children go to the school in their own local district. Parents of children in poorer districts adjacent to schools that are better supported have wondered why there is such a difference in schools. These questions have led states to consider ways to equalize educational opportunity. In general, solutions have not included deviating from the local school district idea often because of the implications, especially loss of local control of community schools. Some legislators have turned to the idea of issuing vouchers. This system gives parents a voucher to pay for the tuition (or part of the tuition) for any school, private or public. Parents would then vie for their children's entrance in the desired school and, in turn, the school would choose the most desirable students. Such an arrangement raises questions of how to establish fair and equitable management and who would have the responsibility and power over that management. Another question involves the matter of public support for religious schools, if the chosen school were to be religiously based. Public support for religious education would violate the principle of separation of church and state and alter the idea that citizens in general should support schools, draining monies away from the public schools and making education strictly a personalized, individualized matter rather than both societal *and* personal.

Within the public school framework, charter schools have been created in many states. A charter school differs from a regular public school largely because it is free from many of the restrictions placed on regular public schools and, as a result, can develop innovations. Each charter school will have its own characteristics, often providing special programs and special environments. The development of these schools is meant to provide choice for some students, but not to offer a substantial change in American schooling. (For results of charter schools in California and Minnesota, see the study conducted by Buechler, 1996, for the Indiana Educational Policy Center.)

Although states have passed laws requiring compulsory school attendance, usually until age fourteen, there are provisions for parents to "home school" their own children or enroll them in private schools. Home schooling has been the norm over the years in remote or isolated places such as Alaska, but now home schooling is often being done because of dissatisfaction with existing schools or disagreement with the purposes of schools. Often home schooling takes place through the elementary years and then students enter regular high schools.

Even though our framework for assessing a high school in this book has been constructed with public high schools in mind, the effectiveness categories are appropriate for any schooling.

RESEARCH STUDIES AND REPORTS ON EFFECTIVE SCHOOLS

Good assessments of schools begin by asking significant questions—ones that relate to the really critical aspects of schools. Although there are many ways to establish what is significant, an inquirer should find out what others think and have found to be significant. To this end, what follows is a description of the significant aspects of several school effectiveness research studies and national reports concerning schools. These studies and reports are then analyzed to identify common characteristics of effective schools. From this analysis, a practical framework will be derived. This derived framework will form the basis for identifying an effective school. In this framework, two kinds of information are important: (1) publicly available data that need to be categorized to be helpful in deciding whether or not a school is effective, and (2) the kind of personal observations needed to be made locally. Both publicly available data and information collected by an on-site visit will be merged to construct an assessment framework you can use when considering a particular high school.

William Firestone, Robert Herriott, and Bruce Wilson, reporting on research conducted through Research for Better Schools, Inc. (Firestone, Herriott, & Wilson, 1984), suggest that factors applicable to elementary schools may not apply to secondary schools because of differences in basic organizational structure. The secondary school, when contrasted with the elementary school, has "structural looseness," departmentalization, and increased size. These factors were found to undermine agreement on educational goals and block efforts of administrators to influence classroom management. In addition, secondary schools attend to immediate preparation for "the outside world." More than simply basic skills development must be considered. The curriculum offerings, for example, become critical. Because of the recognized differences between elementary education and secondary education, secondary school effectiveness research will be used to identify the commonly found elements of effective schools.

The Trump Report

The National Association of Secondary School Principals established, in 1956, a Commission on the Experimental Study of the Utilization of the Staff in the Secondary School. J. Lloyd Trump, Associate Secretary of the National Association of Secondary School Principals, was appointed director of the commission. With financial support from the Fund for the Advancement of Education and the Ford Foundation, the commission worked over a four-year period with nearly 100 junior and senior high schools across the nation to develop guidelines to improve secondary schools despite an acute shortage of teachers. J. Lloyd Trump and Dorsey Baynham published the results of the project as a guide to better schools in 1961.

The commission concluded that all their ideas for improving schools have a common characteristic. They demand flexibility in all school arrangements, scheduling, facilities, architecture, staff use, and organization of instruction. Specific characteristics of the average American high school of the future, according to the report, will be as follows. (1) Some classes will be smaller, having perhaps fifteen or fewer students especially for small-group discussion. (2) There will be many opportunities for independent study, providing for differences in individual interests and abilities, and students will be supported with materials and special rooms for independent work (e.g., science, math, languages, arts, etc.). (3) Some classes will be larger, perhaps having as many as 100 to 150 students for presentations in a large-group setting. (4) The three instructional settings will be related and coordinated by a teaching team. (5) Through team teaching and the use of teacher assistants, new staffing patterns, including the use of staff specialists, will replace the unitary autonomous teacher. (6) School facilities will support the flexible and varied requirements of the educational plan. (7) Schedules will be more flexible by having the day arranged in 15- to 20-minute modules with teachers and counselors scheduling students according to educational needs, in 12 hours of large-group instruction per week and in 6 hours of small-group instruction, and 12 hours per week in independent study. Schedules would be made for individual students. (8) Through a focus on inquiry learning, the individual differences of students will be recognized. (9) Differences in teachers will be recognized by differentiated assignments and workloads, involvement in team teaching, and salary differentials related to preparation, experience, and assignment. (10) Recruiting, screening, and education of professional teachers will be a shared responsibility of secondary schools and higher education. (11) Recognized functions of teachers will help establish teaching as more of a profession. (12) Through curriculum organization, students will attain the highest levels of basic skills of which they are capable and go beyond to develop skills and practices of intellectual inquiry, having differing points of entry and exit from educational levels determined by professional decisions, not simply according to age or by amassing credits. (13) A more comprehensive system of evaluation will gauge student performance using a variety of measures, relate school accomplishments to its purposes in evaluating the school, and assess the curriculum according to whether it is accomplishing its aims for all students. (14) Increased communication with the public will make the public closer to the school. (15) Through careful deployment of funds for educational purposes and smart use of facilities and personnel, schools will make funds go farther. (16) Principals will be educational leaders, spearheading research and involvement in educational decisions (Trump & Baynham, 1961).

Conant's Studies

Forty-one years ago, James B. Conant published a report titled *The American High School Today: A First Report to Interested Citizens*. It described the results of a study of public secondary education in the United States and included numerous recommendations (Conant, 1959). Schools across the nation responded to the report's suggestions. In a second report, Conant described opportunities for studying various subjects in 2,000 American comprehensive high schools of medium size. The findings indicated that there was a wide disparity between schools in terms of providing equality of educational opportunity and that inadequate finances spell an unsatisfactory school. He concluded, however, that an excellent comprehensive high school can be developed in any school district that can have at least 750 students in a high school and support it with sufficient funds. He also reported that the study indicated a correlation between quality of the school and relative size of the staff. Furthermore, he suggested that a comprehensive high school should as a minimum meet five criteria:

1. Provide instruction in calculus;
2. Provide instruction in a modern foreign language for four years;
3. Arrange the schedule so that a student may study in any one year English, mathematics, science, a foreign language, social studies, physical education, art or music;
4. Provide one or more advanced placement courses;
5. Have enough English teachers so that the average pupil load is 120 or less. (Conant, 1967)

Goodlad's Study

Of the several monumental studies of American schools conducted in recent years, perhaps the most prominent is "A Study of Schooling," conducted by John L. Goodlad and reported in the book, *A Place Called School* (Goodlad, 1984). Supported by the Spencer Foundation, Ford Foundation, Kettering Foundation, and Danforth Foundation, Goodlad assembled an advisory group of outstanding educators chaired by Ralph Tyler, along with an institute staff. Three years were spent in conceptualizing the study and preparing ways to collect data. Then five more years were devoted to collecting and analyzing data and preparing reports. The topics of thirty-five technical reports that were prepared indicate the depth of exploration in the study. These reports span student and teacher perceptions, summaries of classroom observations, studies of constructs and observation systems, school policies, and other practices.

From this study ten aspects of schooling were identified as common themes. Goodlad and his associates found that as they studied schools these particular aspects of schooling emerged as critical ones. Their report raises many questions about the typical school in terms of the ten themes and discusses the nature of problems associated with them. These are important themes to consider when assessing schools: (1) School functions (the school should emphasize what it considers its important tasks); (2) Relevance of school in the lives of students (students should be able to satisfy their interests and find learning meaningful and the school should be cognizant of the changes in values of the young); (3) How teachers teach (they should be departing from textbooks and using multiple resources); (4) Circumstances of the workplace (teachers should have time to plan, there should be opportunities for teachers to develop intellectually, and students should have opportunities to use nonformal and informal educational resources of the entire community); (5) The curriculum (facts should be used to understand concepts and not studied in isolation or for their own sake, and students should experience the study of subjects and subject matter as struggles and satisfactions of personal development); (6) Distribution of resources for learning (the allocation of teachers to subjects should be deliberately rational and the stress given to particular subjects should be reflected in the school's stated goals and be in concert with the public's view of the school); (7) Equity of access to knowledge (all students including poor and minority students should have the same access to knowledge as other students); (8) Actual values being taught (students should be involved in making moral judgments and understanding the difference between these and decisions based on scientific facts); (9) Satisfaction of students, teachers, administrators, and parents; (10) Awareness of school strengths, weaknesses, and problems.

Boyer's Study

A Carnegie Foundation project, under the direction of Ernest Boyer, conducted another major study of the American high school (Boyer, 1983). A national panel of teachers, principals, superintendents, university administrators, parents, school board members, and citizen representatives was convened to help visit schools, review findings, and formulate proposals. After the foundation's staff reviewed the literature and made some visits to schools and talked with educators from many sectors of the education community, fifteen schools were selected for study. These schools were chosen to represent a cross section of American public secondary education. A team of twenty-five educators visited the selected schools, with visits scheduled for twenty school days at each institution. The project's aim was to stimulate discussion about secondary education and reaffirm the nation's historic commitment to public schools. The report was published as *High School: A Report on Secondary Education*, with Ernest L. Boyer as author.

The report proposes four essential goals for high schools and then presents ways to accomplish them. The goals, given here in paraphrased form, are as follows: (1) helping all students develop the capacity to think critically and communicate effectively; (2) having students learn about themselves through a core curriculum based on human experiences common to all people; (3) preparing all students for work and further education through electives to develop individual aptitudes and interests; (4) aiding all students to fulfill social and civic obligations through school and community service.

From this study a number of proposed priorities for effective schooling emerged: (1) To have a clear and vital mission (i.e., clear goals); (2) To have a program that helps all students become skilled in written and oral use of English (stressing the centrality of language in the curriculum and its national and global context); (3) To have a core of common learning; (4) To prepare students for a lifetime so that they can move with confidence from school to both work and further education; (5) To enable students to engage in social and civic service activities; (6) To have good working conditions for teachers and strengthen the profession; (7) To have effective classroom instruction; (8) To provide technology linked to teaching and learning; (9) To have flexibility in school size and use of time making available new learning places in the school; (10) To reduce bureaucracy and give support to principals so that they can be effective leaders; (11) To have connections with higher education and corporations; (12) To be supported by parents, school boards, and government, affirming commitment to public education (Boyer, 1983).

Wilson and Corcoran's Study

Bruce Wilson and Thomas Corcoran of Research for Better Schools reviewed information on the first three years of the federal government's secondary school recognition program, 1983–85, and derived outstanding characteristics and comparative strengths of the schools selected for recognition. A total of 571 secondary schools had been selected as exemplary institutions representing urban, suburban, and rural communities across the United States. Researchers found five outstanding characteristics of those schools compared to high schools nationally. The schools had larger enrollments, there were almost as many newly appointed principals as experienced principals, there were no significant increases in graduation requirements, none of the schools reported attendance below 90 percent, and more schools encouraged students to pursue higher education. The exemplary institutions, compared to schools nationally, had greater strengths in the following areas: (1) satisfactory student discipline; (2) more extracurricular participation; (3) recognition of good student behavior and performance; (4) good school climate; (5) high rates of student and teacher attendance; (6) more time spent on academics; (7) teacher efficacy (effectiveness); and (8) good community support (Corcoran & Wilson, 1986).

In an earlier study of the first two years of the national secondary school recognition program, Wilson and Corcoran found that the successful schools exhibited nine characteristics: (1) clearly defined and agreed-on school goals; (2) high expectations of student achievement; (3) a high level of professional collaboration within the school; (4) positive and open relationships between teachers and students; (5) good management of change; (6) strong institutional leadership; (7) a high level of community involvement with the school; (8) a high level of extracurricular participation; and (9) a balance between control and delegation in the school's operation (Corcoran & Wilson, 1985).

Considering these two studies together, it is suggested that the following aspects of exemplary schools emerge, not in order of importance: (1) good school climate, including positive and open relationships between teachers and students, a strong work culture with high productivity, satisfactory student discipline, and high rates of student and teacher attendance; (2) good community involvement and support; (3) high expectations of students, including more time spent on academics and recognition of good student achievement and behavior; (4) a high level of extracurricular participation; (5) teacher efficacy or effectiveness including a high level of professional collaboration; (6) clearly defined and agreed-on school goals; (7) strong institutional leadership, including good management of change and a balance between control and delegation.

Gable's Report

In a paper presented at the National Meeting of the National Council on Measurement in Education, April 1986, Robert K. Gable and others offered details of the development of a questionnaire on parent attitudes toward school effectiveness. What makes this work important is that six categories were identified in their study concerning school effectiveness and these categories provide another indication of what constitutes an effective school. The categories were derived from reviews of the literature on school effectiveness, teacher questionnaires used in the "Connecticut Secondary School Effectiveness Project," and an expert panel. The six categories are: (1) good school–community relations; (2) clear school mission; (3) high expectations (of students); (4) safe and orderly environment; (5) good instructional leadership; (6) frequent monitoring of student progress.

Ogden and Germinario's Study

Based on the U.S. Department of Education's Blue Ribbon School Program, Evelyn Hunt Ogden and Vito Germinario identified several aspects of schooling that promote student learning (Ogden & Germinario, 1995). These aspects include: (1) school organizational vitality; (2) effective planning and school leadership; (3) productive teaching; (4) productive student environment; (5) parent and community support and involvement; (6) organization, planning, funding, and instructional practice especially in language arts, mathematics, social studies, science, the arts and preparation for life in the Information Age.

The Shopping Mall High School

Another influential report was issued in 1985. Cosponsored by the National Association of Secondary School Principals and the Commission on Educational Issues of the National Association of Independent Schools, three researchers spent three years visiting fifteen high schools. The report was developed from analyses of their field notes from interviews and classroom observations. Results of the study were published as *The Shopping Mall High School*; it was the second book to emerge from a five-year secondary school inquiry, the first book being Theodore Sizer's *Horace's Compromise: The Dilemma of the American High School*.

Using the shopping mall metaphor as a way of looking at high schools, Arthur G. Powell, Eleanor Farrar, and David K. Cohen focused on the relative effectiveness of schools on particular students, noting that a school is rarely either effective or ineffective for all those enrolled. They found schools to be characterized by most students having modest interest in academic work, most teachers having heavy workloads, many teachers having modest competence, most schools celebrating tolerance, and schools having virtual neutrality about the quality of academic work. The shopping mall concept of a high school works well, according to the report, because the school has a variety of course offerings with choice among them and it exhibits neutrality about the value of the offerings. Students who want to learn are able to do so and parents can demand special courses or activities. However, many students, especially "average" students, through avoidance of rigorous courses and lack of parents' insistence on special treatment, do not learn adequately, yet go on to graduate. These students are not pressed to develop character and conduct nor pushed to learn and care about learning. In short, the special offerings may allow students to feel satisfaction and even success without really learning to use their minds. The authors then describe the historical background of how these characteristics came to be. In conclusion, the researchers make several suggestions that will be of interest to those concerned about good schools.

According to the authors of *The Shopping Mall High School*, informed consumers (parents and students) should know when variety, choice, and neutrality—the very salient characteristics of the high school—make many average students nonspecial, trouble-free, invisible, and taken for granted. To overcome this problem, schools need to convert as many students as possible to special status and this requires skilled teachers who will be their advocates and will not settle for avoidance of learning. Special courses must be developed and cleverly and aggressively marketed to currently nonspecial students. Teachers must expect students to do more than students think they can or say they will and then keep after them to perform well. Personal attention should not be confused with individualization that is anonymous. Families of students need to develop a commitment to the school and knowledge about what is happening.

To organize a school so that it emphasizes academic purpose, high expectations of students, and personalization the report suggests that teachers need to accommodate differences in how students learn and recognize that every teenager is in some sense special. If teachers had lighter loads, lessons could be better planned, less routine, and more effective. Less conventional classes would allow students to engage in more productive work with closer teacher attention. There would be more time for conversations between teachers and students as well as for conversations between teachers as they engage centrally in educational decision making (Powell et al., 1985).

Breaking Ranks Report

In 1996 the Carnegie Foundation for the Advancement of Teaching and the National Association of Secondary School Principals cooperatively prepared a report envisioning the high school of the twenty-first century, *Breaking Ranks: Changing an American Institution*, and an executive summary of the report. Over a two-year period, a national commission composed primarily of educational practitioners with varied backgrounds and extensive knowledge of what schools face in the twenty-first century prepared the report designed to promote change in American high schools. The eight high school principals, an assistant principal, two teachers, two students, a central office administrator, two college professors, a senior fellow of the Carnegie Foundation, and senior staff members of the National Association of Secondary School Principals formed the commission. They drew on their personal knowledge and experience and upon the research base of the two organizations to prepare the report. The report's conclusions include nine stated purposes of the high school and a number of recommendations that relate to those purposes. Six main themes in the set of recommendations were identified.

The following purposes of the high school represent the commission's vision of the American high school in the twenty-first century (paraphrased): (1) To be a learning community expecting demonstrated nationally comparable academic performance of students; (2) To get students ready for their next stage of life; (3) To provide students with many options; (4) To prepare students as lifelong learners; (5) To teach good citizenship for full life in a democracy; (6) To help students develop socially as well as academically; (7) To provide a foundation for students to participate successfully in a technological society; (8) To equip students for interdependency with others; (9) To unabashedly advocate on behalf of young people.

The *Breaking Ranks* report identified the following six themes as ones that characterize good high schools: (1) personalization (e.g., breaking the school into units of no more that 600 students, giving students teacher advocates, and individualizing the curriculum); (2) coherency (e.g., creating more interdisciplinary study to promote better understanding); (3) time flexibility (e.g., flexible scheduling including lengthening the school year and modifying the Carnegie unit); (4) technology (using technology throughout teaching-learning); (5) professional development of teachers and leaders (updating and improving instruction and academic leadership); (6) school leadership (recognizing and benefiting from good leadership in the school).

The commission's recommendations are in three sections, each having subcategories and then specific recommendations. What follows is a brief description of those recommendations.

The first set of recommendations relates to how the high school should construct itself. The curriculum should offer essential knowledge, integrate it, and make connections to real life. Teachers should be well prepared and use a variety of instructional strategies to engage students in their own learning. The entire school should have a climate conducive to teaching and learning. Technology should be employed throughout the school and integrated into all aspects of the curriculum. Space and time should be structured for flexibility (e.g., flexible scheduling, small units to banish anonymity, and full-time teachers with no more than ninety students a term). The school should assess individual student, collective, and institutional outcomes.

The second set of proposals relates to the web of support for a school. There should be professional development (a learning community) that helps school staff fulfill their potential. There should be an understanding of and respect for diversity in its broadest sense throughout the school. Governance should result in the capacity of each school to engage in school-level change and have responsibility for implementing policies. Resources should be furnished as determined by the learning goals of the school. The school must establish ties with institutions of higher learning. There should be strong and positive relationships among teachers, students, and others in the school and links should be formed with parents, public officials, community agencies, businesses, neighboring schools, and others in the outside community.

The third set of proposals relates to having good school leadership. The principal's role should be pivotal, but leadership must draw on the strengths of teachers and others in the school (*Breaking Ranks*, 1996).

Coalition of Essential Schools' Principles

Founded in 1954, a project in secondary school reform emerged from the Study of High Schools chaired by Theodore Sizer. The project developed into a coalition of secondary school educators committed to grassroots restructuring of schools. The group promotes shared decision-making and autonomy at the local level, but is guided by several fundamental principles that are of particular significance in identifying good schools. The Coalition of Essential

Schools lists ten common principles of an effective school based on the writings of Theodore Sizer, especially *Horace's School: Redesigning the American High School*, and listed at the Essential Schools internet site, *http://www.essentialschools.org*. These common principles follow (paraphrased briefly): (1) There should be a focus on helping young people learn to use their minds well (the central intellectual purpose of the school); (2) Students should master a limited number of essential skills and areas of knowledge shaped by the intellectual and imaginative powers and competencies needed by students; (3) Goals should apply to all students and be tailor-made to every group or class of students; (4) Teaching and learning should be personalized; (5) Students should be considered students-as-workers and teachers as coaches; (6) Teaching and learning should be assessed on student performance of real tasks; (7) Stress should be on values of unanxious expectation, trust, and decency; parents should be key collaborators and vital members of the school community; (8) The principal and teachers should be generalists first, specialists second, and have a commitment to the whole school; (9) Administrative and budget targets should include limited student loads per teacher, time for collective teacher planning, competitive salaries, and reasonable per pupil cost; (10) The school should be nondiscriminatory and inclusive, modeling democratic practices, honoring diversity, and challenging inequity (Coalition of Essential Schools, 2000).

Teddlie and Stringfield's Research

The identification of effective schools began in earnest after a U.S. Office of Education study by J.S. Coleman and associates reported that schools bring little influence to a child's achievement that is independent of the child's background and general social context. In other words, schools don't matter because the critical factors related to student achievement are not factors that schools control (Coleman et al., 1966). Since the Coleman report, defining effective schools as ones in which there is essentially no relationship between family background and achievement and identifying factors that characterize effective schools have become known as school effects research (Teddlie & Stringfield, 1993).

The results of school effects research, according to Teddlie and Stringfield, clearly show that schools, indeed, do make a difference in student achievement. In their ten-year study of the effects of schools with differing student body socioeconomic status, characteristics of effective and ineffective middle and low socioeconomic status schools were identified. They found four school characteristics of effective schools regardless of socioeconomic status: (1) clear academic mission and focus; (2) orderly environment; (3) high academic engaged time-on-task; (4) frequent monitoring of student progress. However, several characteristics of effective schools depended on socioeconomic status. For example, in effective middle socioeconomic schools, teachers held very high present and future educational expectations of students and deemphasized external rewards for academic achievement, while in effective low socioeconomic schools, teachers held high present but modest future educational expectations, and emphasized external rewards for academic achievement. Teddlie and Stringfield suggest that school plans should take into account the entire social context of the school and not rely on a simple listing of generic school effectiveness characteristics. Schools in different contexts require different strategies for success (Teddlie & Stringfield, 1993).

Good and Brophy, two educational researchers, conducted a review of school effectiveness studies whose results confirm the significance of factors identified in the studies previously described. They found the following characteristics consistently observed in effective schools:

1. strong academic leadership that produces consensus on goal priorities and commitment to instructional excellence;
2. a safe, orderly school climate;
3. positive attitudes toward students and expectations regarding their abilities to master the curriculum;
4. an emphasis on instruction in the curriculum (not just filling time or on nonacademic activities) in allocating classroom time and assigning tasks to students;
5. careful monitoring of progress toward goals through student testing and staff evaluation programs;
6. strong parent involvement programs;
7. consistent emphasis on the importance of academic achievement, including praise and public recognition for students' accomplishments (Good & Brophy, 1991, p. 442).

Differences in American High Schools

By its very nature American education is varied. To describe a typical high school would be tantamount to describing the weather of the United States at any given time, realizing just how varied the weather is from north to south and east to west. States differ in educational perspectives and needs as much as countries do in Europe. It is expected that high schools will be different from one another and that each strives to identify its own mission and its own strengths and weaknesses. On the other hand, the studies on effectiveness have provided commonalties permitting the construction of a framework that can be used to find if a particular high school is effective. This framework, however, does not imply nor is it suggested that high schools become uniform. It will offer a way to recognize differences that will suggest the best fit of a student in a particular school. Ernest Boyer, commenting on his report on secondary education in American, states, "There are many ways by which excellence is achieved. Strategies to improve public education will differ from one school to another, and many points of view, constructively presented, can only enrich the quality of the debate and, ultimately, the quality of education" (Boyer, 1983, p. xiv).

SCHOOL EFFECTIVENESS CATEGORIES

Considering these key studies and reports on what constitutes an effective school, and keeping in mind the historical sweep of the evolution of purposes of the public high school in the United States, several aspects of schooling are suggested as fundamental and useful categories to use in evaluating any particular high school:

1. Organizational and administrative vitality/effectiveness
2. Instructional environment
3. Richness of the curriculum
4. Academic achievement
5. Support for learning
6. Student life
7. Parent/community relations

It will be suggested in Chapter 3 that on entering a school you will begin to sense its climate. To provide some background to enable you to more fully sense school climate, what follows are general school climate factors identified in 1973 by about 200 school administrators from across the nation. The ideas and observations of these administrators were analyzed by a committee of educators chaired by Robert S. Fox, then Director of the ERIC Clearinghouse for Social Studies/Social Sciences Education, Boulder, Colorado, and reported in a Phi Delta Kappa publication, *School Climate Improvement: A Challenge to the School Administrator*. The first factor is respect. Do students, teachers, and administrators see themselves as persons of worth? There should be no or little evidence of put-downs. Second, do members of the school community trust one another? There should be evidence that people can count on one another to be honest and not let each other down. Third, there should be high morale. Fourth, do people have a voice in what is being decided? There should be opportunities for all to contribute ideas and have them considered. Fifth, do members of the school community see continuous academic and social growth? There should be evidence of such growth. Sixth, is there cohesiveness? Students, teachers, and administrators should feel part of the school. Seventh, is the school involved in self-renewal or it is just following routines? There should be evidence of change, but with low stress and conflict. Eighth, is the school a caring institution? There should be signs that everyone feels that someone is concerned about him or her as a human being (Fox, 1974).

What follows is a presentation of the school effectiveness categories, each containing aspects from the various studies and reports related to the particular category. This analysis will identify aspects that not only come from research and study, but also will show the most recurring aspects in the research. Table 1.1 contains brief phrases or words that identify features of effective schools studies so that the whole scope of the analysis can be seen and quick reference made to trace any identified aspect of effective schooling to its research base. Appendix A presents the categories in outline form, along with the kinds of information normally available that are related to each of the categories.

Does the School Have Organizational and Administrative Vitality/Effectiveness?

Probably the aspect of schooling most cited in the research as a characteristic of effective schools is that of the school having a clear idea of its mission. Trump concluded that good schools have stated goals and those goals are used in evaluating the success of the curriculum or the whole school. Goodlad indicates that the effective school states what it considers its most important tasks and relates school decisions such as allocation of teachers to subjects to the goals. Boyer adds that the effective school's mission is clear and vital. Wilson and Corcoran not only stress clarity in stating school goals but indicate that effective school goals are agreed on by those who are affected by them. The Coalition of Essential Schools indicates that the central purpose of the effective school is that of educating students so that they will use their minds well. In addition, the coalition finds that goals must apply to all students and be tailor-made to every group or class of students if the school is to be effective. Teddlie and Springfield's research supports having a clear academic mission and focus as a critical factor in an effective school. As will be shown in Chapter 2, school mission statements and/or stated goals can be secured for schools you wish to assess, and Chapter 3 will provide questions to ask related to the school's mission when you make an on-site visit. Chapters 2 and 3 will also address each of the effectiveness categories.

Another critical factor identified in the research on school effectiveness related to the school's organizational and administrative vitality and effectiveness is that of strong leadership. Trump indicates that the principal must be an educational leader, spearheading research and being immersed in academic decision-making. Boyer's study concludes that the school's bureaucracy must be minimal to permit the principal to be an educational leader and that support must be given to enable this to take place. Wilson and Corcoran's study found that strong instructional leadership characterized by good management of change and a balance between control and delegation is a critical factor in good schools. Gable's study affirms good instructional leadership as critical and Ogden and Germinario add that the leadership must engage in effective planning and demonstrate organizational vitality. *Breaking Ranks* identifies good school leadership as critical and the role of the principal as pivotal and that the leaders should draw on the strengths of others in the school; it adds that school leaders should be involved in their own professional development. The Coali-

Table 1.1
Analysis of Effective School Factors

Study/category	Organizational and Administrative Vitality/Effectiveness	Instructional Environment	Richness of Curriculum	Academic Achievement	Support for Learning	Student Life	Parent/Community Relations
Corcoran & Wilson (1985)	Clearly defined and agreed-on goals. Management of change. Strong institutional leadership. Balance between control and delegation.	High teacher attendance. High level of professional collaboration.			Good community support.	Good climate. Strong work culture. Satisfactory discipline. Open student-teacher relationships.	High level of commitment and involvement of parents.
Goodlad (1984)	School functions stated. Awareness of strengths/weaknesses. Satisfaction of administrators.	Good working conditions. How teachers teach. Equity of access to knowledge.	Facts used to know concepts. Equity of access to curriculum.		Distribution of resources according to school goals.	Relevance of school in lives of students. Satisfaction of students.	Satisfaction of parents.
Boyer (1983)	Clear & vital mission. Principal as effective leader. Flexibility in school size & use of time.	Good working conditions for teachers. Effective classroom instruction.	Skilled in written & oral English. Core of common learning.	Student achievement test for advisement.	Apparent public commitment.	Confidence from school to work & further education.	Students engage in social and civic activities.
Ogden & Germinario (1995)	School organizational vitality. Effective planning and school leadership.	Productive teaching. Instructional practice in language arts, math, social studies, science, arts and information.	Organization & planning in language arts, math, social studies, science, arts and information.			Productive student environment.	Parent and community support.

Source							
Gable (1986)	Clear school mission. Safe and orderly environment. Good leadership.	High expectations. Instructional leadership.		Frequent monitoring of student progress. High expectations			Good school/community relations.
Coalition of Essential Schools (2000)	Principal and teachers have sense of commitment to entire school. Goals apply to all students.	Personalized instruction attending to individual interests. Instruction in hands of teachers and principal.	Curriculum decisions guided by student input. Focus on using minds well.	Academic achievement is the central intellectual purpose. Students master a limited number of essential skills and areas of knowledge. Student performance of tasks is central.	Independent and remedial study for those who need it.	There is significant social and emotional development.	Families are vital members of the school community with close collaboration.
Breaking Ranks (1996)	Professional development of teachers and leaders. School has units of no more than 600 students.	Flexibility in space and time.	Lifelong learners and good citizens. Individualized curriculum. Multiple options.	School is committed to demonstrable academic achievement.	School advocates in behalf of young people. Extensive use of technology.	Students have experiences in transition to next stage of life. Students develop as social beings.	
Trump & Baynham (1961)	Flexibility in scheduling. Principal as educational leader. School evaluation based on goals.	Flexibility in class size, staffing, and type of instruction. Inquiry learning.	Include basic skills and intellectual inquiry development.	Comprehensive student evaluation system.	Facilities should support instruction.	Recognize individual differences.	Close relationship with public. Shared responsibility with colleges. Good communication.
Teddlie & Stringfield (1993)	Clear academic mission and focus. Orderly environment.	High academic time-on-task. Teacher expectation.		Frequent monitoring of student success.			
Shopping Mall (1985)		High teacher expectation.	Make all students special.		Advocates for students.	Students feel special.	Parents are informed consumers. Families are committed to the school.

tion of Essential Schools supports the critical role of the principal as leader and indicates that the principal should be a generalist first, specialist second, and be committed to the whole school.

A safe and orderly environment has been identified in a number of the studies and reports as being an important factor in effective schools. Gable's study identified having a safe and orderly school environment as a characteristic of effective schools. *Breaking Ranks* found that an effective school has a whole-school climate that is conducive to teaching and learning and promotes understanding and respect for diversity. The Coalition of Essential Schools concludes that the effective school is characterized by trust and decency in the behavior of students, administrators, teachers, and others in the school, and that the school's practices model democratic practice, honor diversity, challenge inequities, and are nondiscriminatory and inclusive. Teddlie and Springfield found an orderly environment to be a critical characteristic of effective schools. Fox's report on school climate indicated that the school must be a caring institution in which there is pervasive trusting of one another, a cohesiveness, high morale, and evidence of school members engaging in self-renewal and seeing themselves as persons of worth. All these studies help establish what it means to have a safe and orderly school and that these characteristics are ones associated with effective schools.

Whether or not a school is safe and orderly can be determined by examining school rules and processes (including whether the school keeps track of visitors) and the way students behave inside and outside the classrooms. Violence in schools has been a major media topic in recent years, especially in terms of mass killings, but also in terms of day-to-day situations and threats of violence. The school is only a segment of the larger society and is subject to the same salient activities and mores. A safe and studious atmosphere is normally expected in the school setting. In recent years schools have instituted policies and procedures believed to reduce or eliminate instances of violence. These innovations span a spectrum from programs for students on conflict resolution to detection devices at school entrances. It is now a regular procedure in schools to identify visitors and require the wearing of an identifying badge. Guns and knives are strictly prohibited and violators are disciplined or removed. Police departments often work cooperatively with schools and school counselors increasingly are trained to help reduce violence. Schools now develop plans to promote safe and nonviolent environments and ways to respond quickly to threats of violence. For further information, see *Creating Safe and Supportive Schools: Prevention and Response*, a forthcoming book by Michael A. Wanko.

Flexibility is another characteristic of effective schools according to the examined studies and reports. Trump's study is a forerunner in identifying flexibility as a critical factor in effective schools and suggesting a variety of ways to schedule classes, vary class lengths, and be flexible in the use of staffing by employing the idea of differentiated roles for teachers and others. Boyer found flexibility in use of time, making places available for instruction and study, and school size to be characteristics of a good school. *Breaking Ranks* emphasizes flexibility in scheduling, school year, using other means than the Carnegie unit to assess completion of schooling, and employing small school units to banish student anonymity.

It should be noted that although the factors of having a clear and vital mission, good leadership, a safe and orderly environment, flexibility, and a good school climate have been found to be related to good schools, they do not constitute an exhaustive or absolute guide to evaluating the school's organizational and administrative vitality and effectiveness. By using these factors you can collect and organize data and observations to form a good idea of whether a particular school has organizational and administrative vitality and effectiveness. You will, however, only have examined a sample of the school. Then too, schools in different contexts require different reform strategies (Teddlie & Stringfield, 1993).

Is There an Effective Instructional Environment?

The nature of the school's instructional environment is complex and perhaps that is why many factors emerged from an analysis of the research studies and reports. Several aspects of effective schools, however, stand out and they are as follows: appropriate teacher expectations of students, personalization of instruction, focus on academics, and the conditions of the classroom.

The Coalition of Essential Schools identified the unanxious expectations of students by teachers as a critical factor in effective schools. *The Shopping Mall High School* also cites high teacher expectations as a critical aspect. Teddlie and Stringfield found that teacher expectation in effective schools differed according to the socioeconomic level of the school. Effective lower socioeconomic level schools focused on immediate student expectations especially related to achievement of basic skills using tangible rewards for student achievement. Effective higher socioeconomic level schools focused on both immediate and long-term educational goals and did not develop tangible reward systems. It seems that having appropriate and high expectations of students is an important aspect of a good school.

The personalization of instruction was cited in a number of studies. Trump's study found that students need to be engaged in inquiry activities to personalize their education and that various sized groups of students should meet with teachers, some as small as fifteen students, to permit teachers to know students. Conant emphasized the relationship between quality of instruction (including personalization) and size of the staff (class size and use of teachers with appropriate background for teaching the subject). Conant, as an example of student load being a critical factor, recommends that English teachers have a teaching load of no more than 120 students. *Breaking Ranks*, a later study, recommends no more than ninety students per term for a full-time high school teacher, in order to permit greater personalization of instruction.

The Coalition of Essential Schools identified the personalization of teaching and learning and limited student load per teacher to permit time for planning and collaboration as critical factors in effective schools.

The Coalition of Essential Schools recognized that effective schools focus on helping students use their minds well and that students are assessed on performance of real tasks. Trump found that good schools have a comprehensive system of student evaluation (not just paper and pencil tests). Teddlie and Stringfield found that good schools had students engaged in high academic time-on-task and that there was frequent monitoring of student academic progress.

Several factors related to the circumstances of instruction were identified by Trump's study: flexibility in the use of space, variation in class size (utilizing small-group, large-group, and independent study), and variation in kinds of instruction related to the class groupings. Team teaching was recommended in his report. Goodlad found that circumstances of the workplace of teachers require adequate time for planning, opportunities for teacher intellectual development, and opportunities for students to use nonformal and informal educational resources of the community (i.e., outside the school). Teacher efficacy and a high rate of teacher attendance were found by Wilson and Corcoran to be significant factors in effective schools. Having opportunities for teacher development, especially for updating instruction, was a factor identified in the *Breaking Ranks* study. In that study it also was found that in an effective school teachers are well prepared and use a variety of instructional strategies, engaging students in personal study. Teachers provided students with many learning options and engaged them in activities to equip them for interdependency in the larger world. Teachers also understood and respected diversity as they provided instruction.

In a review of the 1996 report of the National Commission on Teaching and America's Future, Linda Darling-Hammond comments on mathematics test scores. According to her, on an internationally administered test, scores for particular states in the United States were matched with countries from the highest to the lowest averages. "The high scoring states regulate education very little, and none has a statewide testing system, but all three have professional standards for teachers that have enacted rigorous requirements for teacher education and licensing and that refuse to allow districts to hire unlicensed teachers. The lowest-scoring states regulate schools heavily and test students frequently, but they have low standards for teacher education and hire large numbers of unqualified teachers each year" (Darling-Hammond, 1997, pp. 25–27). The report highlights the critical importance of teacher characteristics, especially preparation, in providing effective schooling.

Boyer's report on secondary education in America (Boyer, 1983) concluded that productive teaching is related to the goals and objectives of the instruction and that teachers should ask probing questions. Boyer describes the enduring qualities of a good teacher as follows. "There remain some old-fashioned yet enduring qualities in human relationship that still work—command of the material to be taught, contagious enthusiasm for the work to be done, optimism about the potential of the students (teachers are quite properly eternal optimists), and human sensitivity, that is, integrity and warmth as a human being" (p. 149). His report stresses that instructional effectiveness is related to both good working conditions for teachers and the nature of actual classroom instruction.

Two characteristics of the instructional environment in schools having good student achievement gains have been identified in a review of school effects research by two educational researchers: (1) positive teacher attitudes toward students and expectations regarding their abilities to master the curriculum; (2) an emphasis on instruction in the curriculum (not just filling time or on nonacademic activities) in allocating classroom time and assigning tasks to students (Good & Brophy, 1991, p. 443).

The focus of today's instruction has shifted from simply expecting recall of information and the rote memorization of algorithms (cookbook-type ways to solve problems) to expecting conceptual learning and helping students to think and reason. By conceptualizing, students understand ideas rather than simply learning names for things. Curriculum standards developed by national professional associations highlight demonstrable academic achievement that includes critical thinking and problem solving. This means that state-of-the-art instruction must provide for the development of students' problem-solving abilities and critical thinking processes. Instructional strategies that promote student inquiry and discovery demand more than the traditional lecture-recitation routine. The modern classroom should provide for access to information, including Internet access and other readily available information sources that permit the deep exploration of ideas and hypotheses. Students must have time for discussion and exploration. They must have practice in formulating questions as well as responding to the teacher's questions. Cooperative learning is often utilized in providing for such intellectual interaction and exploration of ideas. Small-group instructional processes in which students work together but are held individually responsible for their own achievement exemplify cooperative learning. A variety of instructional strategies and not just a single way of conducting classes characterize modern classroom instruction.

Another shift of thinking about instruction has resulted in educators applying the concept of multiple intelligences (rather than a single intelligence ladder along which students could be placed in a linear fashion). The Theory of Multiple Intelligences was proposed by Howard Gardner (Gardner, 1983) and has been applied to instruction by recognizing the cognitive diversity of students and, therefore, the need for a variety of instructional strategies to match the diverse student population.

The grouping of students for instruction has been a matter hotly debated ever since specialized courses were developed. As described in the previous presentation of the historical development of purposes of the high school, it is clear that the question of grouping calls into account the purposes of schooling. Many high schools not only group students by self-selection of courses but also by ability. Other schools stress cooperative learning in which the interaction of students of various interests and abilities is valued. The traditional lecture-recitation instructional strategies are not appropriate for cooperative learning settings and, therefore, this increasingly popular classroom strategy requires extensive change in the behavior of teachers as well as students. Just as Horace Mann's recommendations were to change the prevailing lecture-recitation instructional style, cooperative learning is an attempt to move beyond that mode of teaching.

Two very significant aspects of effective schools are evident in the research and recent reports and relate to the student's involvement in the instructional environment. The first is equity to access of knowledge, highlighted in Goodlad's study (1984). This first factor has implications for instruction as well as curriculum. It means that teachers must convey appropriately high expectations for all students and resources must be available for all students to grow academically. The second factor is that students should be active learners or, as Sizer puts it, the learner should be "student-as-worker" (Sizer, 1992). This means that classrooms should be characterized by students often engaged in activities.

In a review of process-outcome research on classroom instruction, Good and Brophy found the following to be the most widely replicated findings concerning teachers. These are the teacher characteristics determined to be related to the highest student achievement test gains (paraphrased): (1) Belief that students are capable of learning and that they can teach them successfully; (2) Most of the classroom time is spent on instruction related to the curriculum; (3) Classrooms are organized to maximize time spent on lessons and learning activities; (4) Students move through the curriculum rapidly but in small steps, minimizing frustration and allowing continuous progress; (5) Teachers engage in active instruction, demonstrating, explaining, and so on, emphasizing concepts and understanding as well as facts and skills; (6) Teachers monitor each student's progress, providing for practice, application, and remedial work; (7) Teachers maintain a pleasant and friendly classroom, being enthusiastic and supportive; (8) Teachers utilize whole-class presentations for new materials and appropriately provide for cooperative small-group and independent activities (Good & Brophy, 1991, p. 443). Although it takes many observations to see these factors in operation, they are presented here to show the range of factors involved in effective classroom instruction.

State education department reports, such as school report cards, normally include information related to, but not necessarily identified as being related to, the instructional environment in school districts. Because each state decides on the particular information to include in its report and the form it will take, it is necessary to extract those bits of information related to instructional effectiveness. In Chapter 2 you will find descriptions of the kinds of information related to instruction contained in such reports.

Is There a Richness of Curriculum?

Three general ideas about the high school curriculum seem to pervade the research studies and reports on effective schools: having a core of common learning with emphasis on intellectual development, providing access to knowledge to all students, and preparing students for the future.

Trump's study found that providing in the curriculum both basic skills development and the development of intellectual inquiry is characteristic of good schools. Conant listed four factors that are identified with an effective school curriculum: providing instruction in calculus (assuming that pre-calculus studies are also available); providing four years of one or more foreign languages; making it possible to study in one year English, mathematics, science, foreign language, social studies, physical education, and art or music; and offering one or more advanced placement courses. Goodlad found that in the curriculum of good schools facts are used to understand concepts and not learned as separate entities. Boyer concluded that an effective school has a core of common learning in which language, especially the centrality of learning both written and oral use of English, is included. Ogden and Germanario developed a list of essential studies in a good school. They found that the following are included in the curriculum: language arts, mathematics, social studies, science, the arts, and preparation for life in the technological age. *Breaking Ranks* emphasized that good schools provide a foundation to students for successful participation in a technological society by integrating technology throughout the curriculum. That study also specified that an effective school offers essential knowledge in the curriculum, provides for the integration of that knowledge (within and across disciplines), and connects knowledge with real life, making it personal to students. The Coalition of Essential Schools noted that effective schools focus on students using their minds well and on the mastery of a limited number of essential skills and knowledge that are shaped by the intellectual and creative powers and competencies needed by the students.

Providing equity of access to knowledge to all students is a central theme of Goodlad's report. Although there is an emphasis in the study on existing differences in opportunities afforded students of different economic, racial, and ethnic backgrounds, there is a clear message that good schools provide equal educational opportunities to all students. The *Breaking Ranks* report makes two connections between the curriculum and good schools: offering students many options (including course and study options), and providing for diversity. *The Shopping Mall High School* study indicates that an effective school provides courses and experiences that help make each student special and does not create a curriculum environment favoring one type of student over another.

In terms of the curriculum of a good school providing emphases on the future, preparing for an increasingly technological society has been identified in the Ogden and Germanario study and the *Breaking Ranks* report. Goodlad's report speaks to preparing students for the future by indicating that good schools involve students in making moral judgments and knowing the difference between making such judgments and scientific decision-making. *Breaking Ranks* states that preparing students for lifelong learning and teaching citizenship for a full life in a democracy are significant aspects of the curriculum of good schools.

Goodlad's report found that it is important to know the actual values taught in a school. This means going beyond simply noting curriculum offerings or examining course descriptions to find out what is actually happening in the classrooms. He stresses that those who have different expectations of schools will have different answers to the question of whether the school teaches what it should. Put another way, the question is always personal when one asks whether the school's curriculum includes those subjects and experiences believed best for a particular student. It is important also to ask if the school provides for the general development of each student. Each school will present its curriculum in a variety of ways including curriculum guides for teachers, program planning guides for students, tests given to students, mission statements, and activities offered (described as either cocurricular or extracurricular) described in printed materials or on the school's internet site. From Goodlad's analysis of what is typically offered, one can compare the curriculum in a particular school to see if it includes what would normally be expected. He found the following offerings to be typical: an English core of courses combining mechanics with literature, literature alone and grammar/composition alone. English electives were offered in journalism, speech and creative writing. Mathematics courses included basic skills, algebra, geometry, trigonometry, and calculus. Social studies typically included American history and government, with electives from a range of subjects including economics, sociology, law, anthropology, psychology, world history, history of the particular state, world cultures, human relations, and regional studies of history or geography. Science offerings of small high schools differed from those of large schools. Small schools offered only physical science, biology, and chemistry. Larger schools offered multiple courses in earth science, biology, chemistry, and physics, often clearly differentiating between college-bound and noncollege-bound students. Foreign language offerings included in the curriculum were Spanish, French, and German in that order. Larger schools had more extensive foreign language courses. Vocational and career preparation offerings included titles such as career planning, homemaking, home economics, and the teaching of occupational skills in such courses as business education, distributive education, industrial arts and the teaching of skills often related to the community (e.g., farming economics, cosmetology, upholstery, auto body repair, etc.).

Recently, specialized schools have resurfaced as a way to provide for specialized studies in high school education. Science and arts schools have existed primarily in cities, with their popularity gaining and then waning over the years. Now with the increased need for specialists in the workplace and in institutions of higher learning, specialized high schools are again gaining favor. The comprehensive high school, however, remains the primary means to accomplish the goals of the American high school. Often comprehensive high schools make agreements with specialized schools, including colleges, so that students may attend the specialized school for appropriate courses not available in the comprehensive high school.

With the advent of networking utilizing computer technology, schools are exploring and developing opportunities for students to link with others, outside the high school, through what is termed "distance learning." This connection to other people and sites opens up many possibilities for students and teachers. Many high schools had previously established working relations with nearby institutions such as vocational institutes or community colleges. These official relations enabled students enrolled in the high school to engage in advanced work and receive advanced credit. Now, distance learning provides an extension of those connections to more distant resources. The challenge to high schools is not simply to provide the necessary technology, but to develop ways in which institutions will relate to one another in terms of working conditions, responsibilities, roles, and so on.

Multicultural education is another hotly debated issue in American schooling as citizens and educators continue to engage in constructive self-evaluation and change. There is no question that a more ethnically diverse student body is increasingly populating schools. In the past, neighborhood schools were largely homogeneous in terms of the backgrounds of students, and questions of proper subject matter for study did not arise in large measure. Immigrants were expected to conform to the perceived norm. Now some educators and others are questioning the Western orientation of content and values embedded in it that forms the base of the typical school's curriculum. Those promoting multiculturalism suggest that the curriculum would be richer and could provide a better base for students' understanding of people having differing backgrounds if the curriculum orientation was not so culturally narrow. Linda Darling-Hammond provides clear reasoning for multicultural studies. "A multicultural approach to education explicitly includes a range of experiences, views and representations of human thought in all aspects of the curriculum, from literature and the arts through science, mathematics, and technology" (Darling-Hammond, 1997, p. 126). Because ways of thinking and arguing vary with culture, the curriculum would include a variety of cognitive styles and philosophical perspectives. Those defending the current largely Western/male orientation express fears of losing American values, those values that have enabled our society to progress and be as successful as it is. A common core of studies for everyone would promote equal preparation and common agreement on what is important so that all would have a common set of experiences. This debate is much deeper than that presented here, but the multicultural nature of our school populations cannot be ignored. On either side, the idea of educating the whole citizenry is clearly recognized.

Effective comprehensive high schools have courses and other offerings that include basic academic offerings but differ in the availability of electives and activities. The offerings of each school must be examined in terms of the special needs/interests of a particular student to assess its adequacy.

Do Students Have Good Academic Achievement?

There is a tacit assumption in the studies and reports on good schools that students will have high academic achievement. Having appropriate and high expectations of students has been discussed previously in terms of instruction and its implication that students should have high academic achievement is obvious. Then too, Fox's study on school climate indicated that evidence of student growth is a critical factor in good schools. Trump's study found that effective schools have a comprehensive system of evaluation. By comprehensive we mean that a variety of means to evaluate the progress of students are employed, not simply the administration of paper and pencil tests. In Gable's study the frequent monitoring of student progress is a factor found in effective schools. Teddlie and Springfield also identified the frequent monitoring of student progress as an aspect of good schools. *Breaking Ranks* reported that good schools expect students to demonstrate academic performance that is nationally comparable and that individual students are assessed on outcomes as well as the students collectively. The Coalition of Essential Schools found that in good schools students are assessed on the performance of real tasks.

Academic achievement can be reported in terms of how well students do based on how others have done (this norm-referenced method has been the typical way achievement has been reported) or it can be reported in terms of how well students meet stated standards. In the past few years citizens and educators across the country have called for the adoption of nationally recognized standards. Standards can be used to determine how well students in any local school measure up to a national standard. The federal government's Goals 2000 program calls for the development of such standards and has resulted in the development and adoption of academic standards in many states. These state standards have often been based on standards created by various national professional associations or academic societies. An example is the National Association of Teachers of Mathematics Standards, the success of which has led to the more general trend to create such standards in other fields. Teachers use the state standards to create a curriculum meaningful to their students yet one also related to established significant concepts and processes. Linda Darling-Hammond suggests that "if standards are to support effective teaching, they must find a *medium grain* form of expression, articulating important educational ideas sufficiently clearly to convey meaning but avoiding over specification in order to give teachers room to make curriculum meaningful to their students" (Darling-Hammond, 1997, p. 229). Effective schools are ones that have been engaged in aligning their curriculum with state and national standards.

State achievement testing normally is directly related to standards written as behavioral objectives. The term "behavioral" means that the behaviors expected in achieving the objectives are made explicit in the objective presentation. When such standards are developed and tested by state departments of education, results are often given in terms of the percentage of students passing according to school district or in some instances by individual school.

Assessment is a major process of knowing about the condition of schools, including program success and achievement of individual students. Typical student achievement assessments use many kinds of measures, but one of the most popular is standardized tests. "Standardized" is the name for tests in which results are given in terms of the distribution of scores of a specifically identified population taking the test (e.g., local district, or region, or nation). Objective testing reached its zenith with the multiple-choice formatted standardized test. The average score, or "mean," is used as the reference for reporting results of the test. This type of test is often referred to as norm-referenced. Still using the same type tests (objective), many educators are turning to "criterion-referenced" tests in which the results are reported in terms of standards predetermined by experts and not referenced to the results of others taking the test. Another trend is the use of performance tests that are quite different in form than paper and pencil ones that are purely objective. "Objective" means that the test can be machine-scored. Performance testing, however, requires subjective scoring (i.e., the scorer must make a judgment) and is increasingly becoming valued as more authentic than multiple-choice tests. By "performance" it is meant that students are involved in a direct demonstration or application of skills, reasoning, and knowledge. The use of portfolios, for example, as the performance device for assessment is one that is gaining ground as a means of evaluating student achievement. Such performance-oriented evaluation schemes are, of course, very labor intensive and therefore expensive to facilitate. Other performance tests such as presenting students with "real" problems in laboratory or field settings, while not new, are now being used more extensively.

Most of the media's descriptions of the effectiveness of schools concentrate on achievement test scores almost to the complete exclusion of other aspects of school effectiveness. A review of the school effectiveness studies and reports clearly suggests that academic achievement along with the other six categories constitute a much more balanced and complete consideration of what makes a high school effective.

Is There Adequate Support for Learning?

Three clusters of factors emerged from an analysis of the studies and reports on good schools: appropriateness of support, sufficiency of support, and kinds of support.

Trump reported that in good schools facilities support desired instructional strategies. That is, instruction is not limited by inappropriate facilities; instead, facilities are designed or altered to support instruction. Boyer's study also made this direct connection between providing support and school goals by reporting that in effective schools technology is linked to teaching and learning. *Breaking Ranks* identifies using technology throughout teaching and learning as a mark of a good school. These studies underscore the idea that good schools provide appropriate support for what is needed.

The availability of technological hardware and software (for teacher and student use), library resources, discipline-related equipment and supplies (e.g., those needed for science laboratories, art, music, etc.), classroom supplies, and appropriate facilities are examples of support needed to make instruction effective. If students are to have access to knowledge, then access to appropriate media is essential. Engaging in the kinds of learning activities that involve exploration and discovery requires enabling resources.

Conant's study found sufficient funding to support education a critical factor in good schools. The Coalition of Essential Schools determined that good schools have a reasonable per pupil cost but support the important aspects of the school, having carefully evaluated what is important. Wilson and Corcoran identified good community support as one of the significant aspects of a good school. Community and corporate support will be discussed later under parent/community relations.

It is not only the availability of equipment, facilities, supplies, and media but also the availability of professional expertise skilled in incorporating resources in the instructional process that is significant in providing support for learning. Powell's *The Shopping Mall High School* report associates the provision of student advocates (teachers and counselors) with good schools. The Coalition of Essential Schools links provision for independent study and remedial study with effective schooling. Schools have been required to care for students with special needs under a number of federal regulations, including education for those with disabilities and bilingual education. The key to making support work well in effective schools is the care given to those who are in need.

One of the themes of the report *Breaking Ranks* is that the school should be an advocate on behalf of young people. The report recommends that teachers serve as student advocates and advisors, referring students to guidance counselors when they see the need. To personalize the school experience, as several of the recent reports suggest, advisory programs need to be established in which teachers, peers (e.g., peer counseling), and guidance counselors work together.

Confidence from school to work and further education was noted as a priority in Boyer's agenda for action. It is a characteristic observed in the ways students interact with guidance counselors and the services made available to them as they work on post-school plans.

Does the School Provide a Good Setting for Student Life?

There are many factors identified in studies of effective schools that seem to be able to be grouped in three areas: relevancy of the school to students, good working relationships in the schools, and a productive school environment.

Relevance of school in the lives of students is a factor identified by Goodlad and is often evident on a visit to the school while observing and interacting with students. One aspect of relevance is when students find their studies personally satisfying and value what they are learning. Another aspect found by Goodlad is that the good school understands the changing values of youth. Trump found that students engaged in inquiries do so following their individual differences and so the school is relevant. Wilson and Corcoran found that effective schools have high rates of student attendance, recognizing that students' finding the school relevant is a factor in attendance rates. The Coalition of Essential Schools links understanding of and respect for diversity with good schools.

Good schools have a good climate with open relationships between teachers and students and satisfactory student discipline, according to Wilson and Corcoran's study. Strong and positive relations among teachers and students with the whole school acting as an advocate for young people was found to be an aspect of effective schools in the *Breaking Ranks* report. Fox's report on school climate lists several characteristics of good schools, including students having high morale, caring for each other, trusting and counting on each other to be honest, and believing that they are persons of worth. The Coalition of Essential Schools identified a student climate of trust and decency as characteristic of good schools.

A productive school environment is a factor noted in the Ogden and Germanario study. Productivity often is observable even in brief glimpses of classes in action, students working in the school library or media center, and even in the way students behave as they are passing in the halls. A productive environment encompasses cocurricular activity as well as academic studies. Wilson and Corcoran linked a strong student work culture with effective schools and the Coalition of Essential Schools lists the climate factor of students acting as workers to be related to good schools. *Breaking Ranks* found that good schools provide for the social and emotional development of students, getting students ready for next stages in life, preparing them for a full life in a democracy, and equipping them for interdependency—all of which should pervade the student life in an effective school.

Are There Good Parent/Community Relations?

All the studies and reports considered in this analysis included good relations with parents and the community as a characteristic of good high schools. Aspects of good relations cited in the studies and reports can be categorized in three general descriptions: those related to good communication, those related to involvement of parents and community with the school, and those related to providing support for the school.

Trump's study cited close relationships with the public, including good communication, as an aspect of good schools. The satisfaction of parents is the factor Goodlad established in his study of effective schools. This kind of personal satisfaction is one that contributes to the "word-of-mouth" communication that is so very important, particularly in small communities. Good communication was implied in all the other studies.

Having a high level of parental commitment and involvement is a major aspect of effective schools according to Wilson and Corcoran. Boyer identified school connections with higher education institutions and with corporations as being significant. *Breaking Ranks* found that links formed by a school with parents, public officials, community agencies, businesses, neighboring schools, and others in the community were associated with good schools. The Coalition of Essential Schools found that good schools involve parents as key collaborators and vital members of the school community. Gable's study and Ogden and Germanario's study each identified good school–community relations, including involvement, as a significant factor in good schools. Boyer underscored the importance of the engagement of high school students in community social activities and civic activities. The conclusions of all the studies imply that good schools extend the immediate school community outward into the larger community and involve those beyond the school in their endeavors. Support for the effective high school comes from parents, the school board, and government according to Boyer's study. Powell, in *The Shopping Mall High School* study, cites that in good schools families are committed to the school and parents act as informed consumers.

Effective high schools reach out to the community to establish cooperative activities, and through good working relations and the sharing of accurate information receive appropriate support from the community. In all three of the case studies we present, good relations with the community and good support from the community were hallmarks.

USING THE FRAMEWORK FOR SCHOOL ASSESSMENT

In the next chapters you will find specific ways to gather information within the seven categories that have been developed as a guide to your evaluating schools. Keeping in mind the historical development of the high school in the United States, the purposes and goals of high schools that have been developed over the years and continue to be developed, and the studies of, and reports on, effective schools, you should be able to better sense the significance of the data you gather and the observations you make. You also will be in a better position to understand the context of the mission and characteristics of the particular school you are assessing.

REFERENCES

Aiken, W. M. (1942). *Adventures in American education: Vol. 1. The story of the eight year study*. New York: HarperCollins.

Boyd, J. P. (Ed). (1950). *The papers of Thomas Jefferson: Volume 1: 1760 to 1776*. Princeton, NJ: Princeton University Press.

Boyer, E. L. (1983). *High school: A report on secondary education in America*. New York: Harper & Row.

Breaking ranks: Changing an American institution. (1996). Reston, VA: National Association of Secondary School Principals.

Buechler, M. (1996). *Charter schools: Legislation and results after four years*. Bloomington: Indiana Educational Policy Center.

Button, H. W. & Provenzo, E. F., Jr. (1983). *History of education and culture in America*. Englewood Cliffs, NJ: Prentice-Hall.

Coalition of Essential Schools. (2000). *Ten common principles*. (Online). Http://www.essentialschools.org/aboutus/phil/10cps.html.

Coleman, J. S. et al. (1966). *Equality of educational opportunity*. Washington, DC: U.S. Government Printing Office.

College Entrance Examination Board. (1983). *Academic preparation for college*. New York: The College Board.

Commission on the Reorganization of Secondary Education. (1918). *Cardinal principles of secondary education*. Bureau of Education Bulletin 1918, no. 35. Washington, DC: U.S. Government Printing Office.

Conant, J. B. (1959). *The American high school today*. New York: McGraw-Hill.

Conant, J. B. (1967). *The comprehensive high school: A second report to interested citizens*. New York: McGraw-Hill.

Corcoran, T. B. & Wilson, B. L. (1985). *The secondary school recognition program: A first report on 202 high schools*. Philadelphia, PA: Research for Better Schools.

Corcoran, T. B. & Wilson, B. L. (1986). *The search for successful secondary schools: The first three years of the secondary school recognition program*. Philadelphia, PA: Research for Better Schools.

Cremin, L. A. (1980). *American education: The national experience 1783–1876*. New York: Harper & Row.

Darling-Hammond, L. (1997). *The right to learn*. San Francisco, CA: Jossey-Bass.

Edmonds, R. R. (1979). Effective schools for the urban poor. *Educational Leadership, 37*(10), 15–24.

Firestone, W. A., Herriott, R., & Wilson, B. (1984). *Explaining the differences between elementary and secondary schools: Individual, organizational, and institutional perspectives*. Philadelphia: Research for Better Schools, Inc.

Fox, R. S. et al. (1974). *School climate improvement: A challenge to the school administrator*. Bloomington, IN: Phi Delta Kappa.

Gable, R. et al. (1986). *The development of the pilot form of the parent attitudes toward school effectiveness (PATSE) questionnaire*. A paper presented at the annual meeting of the National Counsel on Measurement in Education, San Francisco, CA, April 1, 1986 (ERIC Document Reproduction Service No. ED 277 733).

Gardner, H. (1983). *Frames of mind: The theory of multiple intelligences*. New York: Basic Books.

George, P S., McEwin, C. K., Jenkins, J. M. (2000). *The exemplary high school*. New York: Harcourt.

Good, T. L. & Brophy, J. E. (1991). *Looking in classrooms*. New York: HarperCollins.

Goodlad, J. I. (1984). *A place called school: Prospects for the future*. New York: McGraw-Hill.

Keefe, J. W. & Howard, E. R. (1997). *Redesigning schools for the new century: A systems approach*. Reston, VA: National Association of Secondary School Principals.

Krug, E. A. (1964). *The shaping of the American high school*. New York: Harper & Row.

Loomis, A. K., Lide, E. S., & Johnson, B.L. (1933). *The program of studies*. National Survey of Secondary Education, U.S. Bureau of Education Bulletin 1933, no.17, Monograph no. 19. Washington, DC: U.S. Government Printing Office.

National Commission on Excellence in Education. (1983). *A nation at risk: The imperative for educational reform*. Washington, DC: U.S. Government Printing Office.

National Education Association. (1894). *Report of the committee of ten on secondary school studies*. New York: American Book Company.

National Science Foundation. (1983). *Educating Americans for the 21st century*. Washington, DC: National Science Foundation.

Nelson, J. L., Palonsky, S. B., & Carlson, K. (2000). *Critical issues in education*. New York: McGraw-Hill.

Ogden, E. H. & Germinario, V. (1995). *The nation's best schools: Blueprints for excellence*. Lancaster, PA: Technomic Publishing Company, Inc.

Powell, A. G., Farrar, E., & Cohen, D. K. (1985). *The shopping mall high school: Winners and losers in the educational marketplace*. Boston: Houghton Mifflin.

Progressive Education Association. (1938). *Progressive education advances*. New York: Appleton-Century.

Pulliam, J. & Van Patten, J. (1995). *History of education in America*. Englewood Cliffs, NJ: Prentice-Hall.

Sizer, T. R. (1984). *Horace's compromise: The dilemma of the American high school*. Boston: Houghton Mifflin.

Sizer, T. R. (1992). *Horace's school: Redesigning the American high school*. Boston: Houghton Mifflin.

Teddlie, C. & Stringfield, S. (1993). *Schools make a difference: Lessons learned from a 10–year study of school effects*. New York: Teachers College Press.

Trump, J. L. & Baynham, D. (1961). *Guide to better schools*. Chicago: Rand McNally.

Turnbull, H. R. & Turnbull, A. P. (1998). *Free appropriate public education: The law and children with disabilities*. Denver: Love Publishing.

Twentieth-Century Fund. (1983). *Making the grade*. New York: Twentieth-Century Fund.

Urban, W. J. & Wagoner, J. L. Jr. (2000). *American education: A history*. New York: McGraw-Hill.

Wanko, M. A. (forthcoming). *Creating safe and supportive schools: Prevention and response*. Monroe Township, NJ: Foundation of Educational Administration.

Wilson, B. L. & Corcoran, T. B. (1988). *Successful secondary schools: Visions of excellence in American public education*. Levittown, PA: Falmer Press, Ltd.

CHAPTER 2

Gathering Education Data

OBTAINING DATA ABOUT SCHOOLS

If you are examining a community for the first time, you may wish to begin with some knowledge of the demographics of the area. Sources listed in Appendix B can guide you to demographic data that will include the ethnic background, educational level, income, occupations, and ages of the population. A good source is the area's chamber of commerce, which can make you aware of the businesses and service organizations (e.g., Women's Club, Kiwanis Club, etc.) that exist in the community, groups that often support the schools. Who are the volunteers in the community and what kind of activities are they engaged in? Is there a community newsletter or local newspaper available to teach you about the community? You might attend a school board meeting or a community meeting. The current activities of the community will give you an understanding of the community's purpose. When you begin your examination of the individual schools, note the school district's mission statement, which should reflect the school's relationship to the community it is serving.

An initial decision about which schools to consider for your child can be made by examining available data about the schools. There may be a school website and/or a "school district profile" or "school report card" produced by the state's department of education. Appendix B includes a website for gaining access to each state department of education. In addition, call the schools you're interested in and ask to have information sent to you. The following types of information were provided to us by the three schools that we visited: descriptive guides to the school's curriculum (which may be referred to as course guides, program planning guides, or curriculum offerings and proficiencies); a school profile; a newsletter distributed to the community; a student/parent handbook; cocurricular activities; policies for school health services and athletic physical policies; or a student handbook.

By reading the case studies of the three schools in Chapter 4, you will notice the difference in the types of data we obtained ahead of each visit. There is a wide difference in the information provided by schools and state departments of education. Despite these differences, we found that it is possible to have a good idea of the school's performance in each of the effective education categories prior to an on-site visit.

NATIONAL, STATE, AND LOCAL DATA

The amount of education statistics gathered from the national to the local level can appear overwhelming. When trying to determine which statistics to focus on, consider the purpose behind the gathering of the information and what the information might be telling you. Keep in mind, too, that although there is an attempt for consistent gathering of statistics at the national level across the states (which has almost been reached), there is always room for statistical error. This serves as a reminder that statistical data about schools is only one element in the identification of an effective school. Be sure to ask questions about any statistical data that you do not understand.

Although there are attempts at the national level to collect information in a uniform way and progress has been made, keep in mind that each state has the authority over its state's educational procedures and that differences exist in the way that information is gathered (e.g., different procedures, different timing) and disseminated. The definitions of statistical data elements included in this section represent the interpretation at the national level. Frequently the state's department of education website will contain descriptions of the data collection process and definitions of what the data represent.

District, state, and national data may be listed together for comparative purposes. By comparing the district data to its state's data one can get an idea of the district's effectiveness. Some states summarize and evaluate their data in a narrative, sometimes noting trends and patterns (see, e.g., Minnesota).

By using the publication *State Comparisons of Education Statistics: 1969–70 to 1996–97* (Snyder & Hoffman, 1998), one can compare state education data for enrollment, pupil/teacher ratios, school expenditures, average daily attendance, and graduation rates. "Care should be used when comparing data from different sources. Differences in procedures, such as timing, phrasing of questions, and interviewer training mean that the results from the different sources are not strictly comparable" (Gerald & Hussar, 1998, p. 179).

This chapter will be arranged in the order of the school effectiveness categories that were defined in the previous chapter. A list of all the categories and the data elements for each appears in Appendix A. Each section that follows will refer to potential data that could be used to assess the effectiveness of a school. Explanations and definitions of many of these data elements are given. We refer you to the annual source published by the National Center for Education Statistics, *Projections of Education Statistics to 2008* (Gerald & Hussar, 1998), for a thorough description of educational statistical data that is gathered and compiled at the national level.

ORGANIZATIONAL AND ADMINISTRATIVE VITALITY/EFFECTIVENESS

Data that is commonly available and helpful in knowing about organizational and administrative vitality and effectiveness includes:

Mission statement
Average daily attendance
Average daily membership
Number of students suspended or expelled
School safety

Mission Statement. High schools should have a published mission statement. We found that the on-site visit was most useful in determining whether a school was living up to its mission statement.

Average Daily Attendance (ADA). Although illness is certainly a justifiable reason for absence from school, an ADA of 90 percent or less should cause concern. A low ADA could be an indicator of a truancy problem or reflect that suspensions or expulsions are assigned at a high rate. Other explanations could include school leadership problems or academic ones, such as ineffective teaching, or a curriculum that is inappropriately serving the students.

The *aggregate days of attendance* is defined as "the sum of days in attendance of all students when school is in session during a given reporting period" (*Derived information related to groups of students*, NCES). The *average daily attendance* is defined: "If not otherwise defined in state laws, the aggregate days of attendance of a given school during a given reporting period divided by the number of days school is in session during this period measured to the nearest half-day. Only days in which the students are under the guidance and direction of school staff members should be considered as days in session. The average daily attendance for groups of schools having varying lengths of terms is the sum of the average daily attendance obtained for individual schools" (*Derived information related to groups of students*, NCES).

Average Daily Membership (ADM). The *aggregate days of membership* is defined as "the sum of the days in membership of all students when school is in session during a given reporting period" (*Derived information related to groups of students*, NCES). The *average daily membership* is defined: "If not

otherwise defined in state laws, the aggregate days of membership of a given
school during a given reporting period divided by the number of days school is
in session during this period measured to the nearest half-day. Only days in
which the students are under the guidance and direction of teachers should be
considered as days in session. The reporting period is generally a given regular
school session. The average daily membership for groups of schools having
varying lengths of terms is the sum of the average daily memberships obtained
for the individual schools" (*Derived information related to groups of students*,
NCES).

Number of Students Suspended and Expelled. The suspension rate refers to
in-school suspension, which will be conducted differently in different schools.
If the suspension rate seems particularly low in comparison with state and national figures, there are several possibilities: exceptionally good behavior, poor
record-keeping, or those who commit the infractions are not being disciplined.

For this statistic it is important to review the definition of the district's
method for collecting and reporting the data. For example, are the suspensions being reported by number of incidents or by number of students? For example, if five students are each suspended three times, which figure is
reported: five or fifteen? This figure should be compared to the ADA. A high
absentee rate could also be an indication of a high and undisciplined truancy
rate if the suspension rate is low.

School Safety. This may be difficult to determine from available data, although some state departments of education do provide detailed school safety
statistics. For example, Arizona lists the following: number of violations of
school and/or district policy involving students and/or non-students; number of students seriously injured (beyond first aid) as a result of a violent act on
school grounds; number of student violations of school or district vio-
lence-prevention policies, which involved the possession and/or use of a
weapon; number of student violations of school or district policies concerning
violence; number of student violations of school or district policies concerning
tobacco, alcohol, and other drugs. The case studies indicate information we
found useful ahead of time—for example, locked facilities, security systems in
existence, dress codes required (e.g., prohibiting "gangwear"-style clothing
and accessories, as in Case Study 3). The on-site visit was most useful in evaluating this area.

THE INSTRUCTIONAL ENVIRONMENT (TEACHERS
AND LEARNERS)

When evaluating the instructional environment, consider the classroom
environment, the teacher, and the learner. We will consider each separately
here.

Classroom

Data available for this area includes:

School enrollment

Class size

Student-teacher ratio

Student mobility rate/enrollment stability

Expenditures

Ethnicity of the student body

Building age

School Enrollment. This is defined as "the number of students registered in a given school unit at a given time, generally in the fall of a year" (Gerald & Hussar, 1998, p. 188). By 2008, enrollment in high schools in all geographic regions is expected to have increased by 15 percent over 1996 (Gerald & Hussar, 1998, p. 4).

Class size has been debated perhaps more at the elementary school level than the high school level. The necessity for smaller classes can be seen especially where individual attention is required (e.g., in a writing skills class or a foreign language class). New Jersey indicates the class size of the homeroom, while Connecticut illustrates the number of students within classes, as, for example, algebra, biology, English or American history. The average secondary class size as of 1993–94 was 23.6 (this figure excludes special education teachers) (Snyder & Hoffman, 1998, p. 60).

The *student/teacher ratio,* different from class size, is defined as "the enrollment of pupils at a given period of time, divided by the full-time-equivalent number of classroom teachers serving these pupils during the same period" (Gerald & Hussar, 1998, p. 189). Some states may give this information in a category labeled *student/staff ratio.* In one state that lists this particular ratio, the following are counted as staff: administrators, classroom teachers, and all other licensed professional personnel. This information, of course, will be very different than a ratio determined exclusively with classroom teachers. If you are comparing school districts in different states and class size is important to you, be sure to note the definitions used by the different states. Snyder and Hoffman (1998, p. 17) claimed that the national average for student/teacher ratio was 17:1. The estimated student/teacher ratio is expected to range between 13.6 and 14.1 by the year 2008 (Gerald & Hussar, 1998, p. 66). This ratio at the district level is different from class size, which will actually be higher. Considered in the teacher portion of the ratio may be those in support of the classroom teachers (e.g., learning disability specialists, resource teachers, or the school library media center specialist).

Questions for you to consider regarding the class size and student/teacher ratio include: How has the district chosen to spend its money? Does the district hire additional teachers in order to maintain a small class size? Is there enough space in the building to hold the additional classes that would be created by smaller class sizes?

Student Mobility Rate. If there is a high incidence of students transferring into and out of the school, this will certainly affect the stability of the school's operation. A frequent turnover in the student population increases the demands on teachers, counselors, and administrative personnel.

Expenditures. Demographics indicate that significant increases in the secondary education population will continue through the early 2000s (Snyder & Hoffman, 1998, p. 13). Because secondary education is more expensive than elementary education, districts will be challenged to meet the increased financial demands.

School districts are funded by federal, state, and local sources. The average breakdown of funding sources for public schools in 1995–96 was 7 percent from federal sources, 48 percent from state sources, 43 percent from local sources, and 3 percent from private sources (Snyder & Hoffman, 1998, p. 22). The responsibility for raising school funds varies among the approximate 15,000 school districts. Local taxes, especially property taxes, can significantly influence the funds available to a school district. State education requirements may affect a local school district's spending ability. For example, spending limits per student may be established by the state, as could minimum teacher salaries or maximum class sizes.

The administrators of a local school district may have limited decisions available to them regarding funding. It is necessary to investigate the method of funding within the state and then within the district. The particular relationship of the school board to the district will influence the methods of funding. How is the school board selected? Are the members elected by the district or appointed? Are the voters able to determine funding policies directly at the polls or through their representative school board member? Are the districts and states applying for all of the state and national funding available? Case Study 3 describes a principal who has been very successful at fund-raising using an entrepreneurial approach.

Expenditures can be listed in several ways: current expenditures, current expenditures per pupil in average daily attendance, expenditures per pupil, total expenditures per pupil in average daily attendance. The following definitions by Gerald and Hussar (1998) represent the definition of each at the national level.

Current Expenditures. "The expenditures for operating local public schools, excluding capital outlay and interest on school debt. These expenditures include such items as salaries for school personnel, fixed charges, student transportation, school books and materials, and energy costs" (Gerald & Hussar, 1998, p. 187).

Current expenditures per pupil in average daily attendance. "Current expenditures for the regular school term divided by the average daily attendance of full-time pupils (or full-timeequivalency of pupils) during the term" (Gerald & Hussar, 1998, p. 187).

The average expenditure per pupil in average daily attendance was $6,146 in 1995–96 and nearly 62 percent of this figure was devoted to pupil instruction (Snyder & Hoffman, 1998, p. 22). Snyder and Hoffman (1998, p. 22) have observed that states are quite consistent in the proportion of per pupil expenditures devoted to instruction. States vary more in the distribution of funding for areas beyond instruction. Snyder and Hoffman (1998, p. 22) discovered the following average breakdown in 1995–96 expenditures:

62%—student instruction

10%—operation and maintenance of school facilities

8%—general and school administration

5%—health, attendance, and speech services

4%—curriculum development, staff training, libraries, media, and computer centers

4%—student transportation

4%—food services

Expenditures per pupil. "Charges incurred for a particular period of time divided by a student unit of measure, such as average daily attendance or average daily membership" (Gerald & Hussar, 1998, p. 188). Some sites list a very specific breakdown. For example, Ohio lists each school's annual spending per pupil by administrative expenditures, building operations expenditures, staff support expenditures, pupil support expenditures, and instructional expenditures.

Total expenditure per pupil in average daily attendance. "Includes all expenditures allocable to per pupil costs divided by average daily attendance. These allocable expenditures include current expenditures for regular school programs, interest on school debt, and capital outlay" (Gerald & Hussar, 1998, p. 190).

Be certain to compare these definitions with the state's method of defining the information. If possible, compare the revenue data over several years. One should note if there appears to be a pattern of decline in funding. This situation may prompt the following questions: How does the decrease compare with other nearby districts and with the state's average? Have the district's taxpayers been responsible for the decrease? Is the district's tax base low? Has there been an enrollment increase without a revenue increase?

Again, compare district expenditures to the state's average to assess the local support. The comparison of instructional expenses, influenced by local revenues, can indicate a community's commitment to its school district. Many factors influence instructional expenses. Consideration, for example, must be given to the cost of serving students with special needs. The identified learning disabled population has increased by 4 percent from 1976 to 1997; from 1986 to 1997 there has been a 35 percent increase in services to disabled students

(Snyder & Hoffman, 1998, p. 15). Small class sizes are a requirement for special needs programs, necessitating additional teachers. Poverty is a factor that influences the amount of financial support needed by a district. According to Snyder and Hoffman (1998, p. 1), poverty is associated with lower student achievement, presenting school districts serving poor families with increased instructional expenses. Another financial challenge for some districts is the number of students with limited English proficiency. Additional programs must be offered to serve both the students and their parents. Although the 1990 national average was 6 percent for those speaking a non-English language at home and not speaking English "very well," some of the larger states carry a much higher percentage of the challenge (Snyder & Hoffman, 1998, p. 3).

Ethnicity of the Student Body. The ethnic description of the student body is frequently available at either the school's website or the state's department of education website. As discussed in Chapter 1, a greater degree of ethnic diversity within a school will expose and prepare students for the broader community in which they may live and work.

Building Age. Two of the schools described in the case studies are older schools that have adapted well to the increased demands of technology, the need for updated science equipment, and demands for adequate athletic facilities. An older building can influence a school's ability to update its resources. If the school you are considering is in an older building, ask how the school has met recent technological challenges.

The Teacher

The teacher is responsible for creating a learning environment for the students, but cannot do that alone. The support offered by the institution and the district, discussed somewhat in the previous section, helps to prepare the working environment for the teacher. The following chapter lists questions to use for a personal assessment of the school's teachers. In addition, the district may provide the following data:

Average years of teaching experience

Teacher salaries

Teacher education (degrees)

Professional development activities

Average Years of Teaching Experience. The average years of teaching experience can vary greatly from state to state. Some see an advantage to a combination of recent graduates and more experienced teachers. In a state by state comparison the average percentage of teaching experience in 1993–94 was 10 percent with three years experience, approximately 60 percent with ten years or more, and approximately 30 percent with twenty years or more experience (Snyder & Hoffman, 1998, p. 17).

Teacher Salaries. The average teacher salary needs to be compared with the years of teaching experience, not just with the average state salary. A "newer" teacher will command a lower salary and vice versa. Although the average national salary in 1996–97 was $38,509 (Snyder & Hoffman, 1998, p. 19), each state is influenced, of course, by cost of living. Even within states, the cost of living of urban and rural districts will influence the salary. A comparison with nearby districts will indicate whether or not the salaries are on par. The salary is an indicator of support by the community for its teachers.

Teacher Education. By 1993–94, almost half the public school teachers had continued their education beyond the bachelor's degree level with advanced degrees (5 percent as education specialists, 42 percent with master's degrees, and 1 percent with doctorate degrees) (Snyder & Hoffman, 1998, p. 17). If the percentage of advanced education for teachers appears to be low, ask if the district offers incentives to the teachers.

Professional Development Activities. This may be indicated by a percentage, as in Case Study 2, or actual professional development opportunities may be listed, as in Case Study 1. We felt the need to ask for more details on-site about this category.

The Learner

For the majority of learner assessment, see the sections on "Academic Achievement" and "Student Life" that follow within this chapter.

Average daily attendance was described in the previous section, "Organizational and Administrative Vitality/Effectiveness." This information can be a reflection of the school's effect on the learner as well as an indicator of the responsibility that the students are taking for their own education.

RICHNESS OF THE CURRICULUM

The entire curriculum may not be available via a school's website although the recommended core requirements may be listed. In both the previous and the next chapters, there is a discussion of specific recommendations at the national level for the high school curriculum. Ask the school to send you a summary of its *curriculum offerings*, normally available to students for course selection in a booklet form, and compare this with the recommendations in Chapter 3 (under the section "Richness of the Curriculum").

Course descriptions vary both in types of courses offered and the amount of description provided. Each school supplies this information using a unique approach. A larger school will, of course, be able to offer a wider course selection. It is important to read the course descriptions to determine the course emphases. In one of our case studies we noted that practice for the PSAT and SAT was embedded in the curriculum. In another case study we noted that the state's standards were included in course descriptions and that the expected proficiencies were clearly listed. One case study listed the anticipated amount of homework. It is possible for a student to have a very clear understanding of the course expectations from reading about the school's curriculum.

Be alert to *Honors* and *Advanced Placement (AP) course offerings* and be prepared to ask the school about its process for developing these offerings to determine the extent to which the school extends instruction to academically achieving students. For example, in one school we were told that most students entered the school with limited foreign language skills so the school did not offer foreign language AP courses until recently, but instead offered a four-year model of offerings. The absence of specific AP courses may have a valid explanation.

School Library Media Center (SLMC). The School Library Media Center is an integrated part of the curricular program and information about its resources may be available either at the state's department of education website or from the school's website. The number of personnel may be given, including both professional and nonprofessional staff. The requirements for professional staffing vary among the states, but the national recommendation by the American Association of School Librarians is for "one or more certified library media specialists working full-time in the school's library media center" (*Position statement on appropriate staffing for school library media centers*). Some states may require a master's degree in library science for the SLMC specialist. Electronic resources made available to students via the SLMC should be linked to the school's website.

Being aware of the curriculum descriptions before visiting the school will prepare you with good questions to ask of specific subject area teachers.

ACADEMIC ACHIEVEMENT

Academic achievement includes, but is not limited to, test scores, which are one indicator—certainly not the sole indicator—of achievement. "Learner outcomes include not only the acquisition of knowledge about traditional subjects, but also the internalization of societal values, such as honesty, tolerance, a sense of community, and teamwork" (Bobbitt, Quinn, & Dabbs, 1992, p. 2). As discussed in the previous section, "Organizational and Administrative Vitality/Effectiveness," the school's mission statement will indicate multiple outcomes expected of its students. A good school serves its community well. Not all students are college-oriented and opportunities for all students to become productive citizens should exist. Thus, if a high school has a large number of students in its vocational program, the overall achievement scores may reflect this since some of these students may not also be in college-preparatory courses.

Recommendations for a more thorough on-site examination of academic achievement are given in the following chapter. Prior to a visit, the following data may be available as indicators of achievement:

Achievement test scores (standardized tests developed at the district, state, or national level)

Percentage of students taking the SAT or ACT

Percentage of graduates enrolled in two-year or four-year colleges

Subjects in which Advanced Placement program courses are offered

Achievement Test Scores. The measurement of student achievement is performed in many ways beyond the predominantly multiple-choice format of standardized tests. The multiple-choice format may elicit a first, quick response instead of a more thoughtful answer. Evidence of academic measurement should include: more than one measure to provide corroboration, more than one kind of testing format, tests that provide sufficient time for performance of cognitive tasks, tests that measure both content and process so that student understanding can be assessed.

A comparison of local, state, and national tests may be given at the state's department of education website. From our experience of exploring school district websites there is often a description of the local or state-developed test. Some concern about locally created tests is that they may be overly focused on the local curriculum. However, nationally designed tests may lack this sensitivity to the variations that exist with curricular and instructional practices. "A single set of measures can be wrong. Given the state of understanding of achievement measurement, investing in different assessment approaches is the most prudent way to collect information that's relevant to policy" (Baker, 1988, p. 13). Although there is concern about the ability of standardized tests to adequately assess student performance, the tests remain as an accountability standard.

Nationally developed tests include the National Assessment of Educational Progress (NAEP), the Scholastic Aptitude Test (SAT), and the American College Testing Program's Assessment (ACT). Since 1969 NAEP has collected the results of its tests given in fourth, eighth, and twelfth grades. Subject areas for the tests include reading, mathematics, science, writing, and history/geography. This is the only national test to track student knowledge and student progress in these subject areas. Reporting is not done at the local level but rather the state level. The results of the ACT and the SAT indicate a level of knowledge in the academic disciplines of English, science, and mathematics and the tests also indicate reading comprehension level. They are intended to measure the degree of academic preparation for college-level work. SAT scores range from 200 to 800 on two parts of the test (verbal and math) with a combined score ranging from 400 to 1600. The ACT score ranges from 1 to 36.

The national average for the SAT in 1998 was 505 for the verbal test and 512 for the math test, for a combined score of 1017.

Percentage of Students Taking the SAT or ACT. School districts are asked by the College Board, which administers the SAT, to encourage as many students as possible to take the SAT. The district results are affected by the number of students taking the test. If a small college-bound group takes the test, the results can be expected to be higher than if all academic levels are included. When a high percentage of the district's students take the test and the results are high, it might be indicative of a strong college-preparatory program by the district. Additional considerations regarding test results are the opportunities that students are given for learning outside school.

Percentage of Graduates Enrolled in Two-Year or Four-Year Colleges. A high percentage of high school graduates who continue their education at the college level can indicate a strong academic program and also reflect an affluent school district. However, a strong college-preparatory curriculum does not necessarily suggest that noncollege-bound students are adequately served.

Subjects in Which Advanced Placement (AP) Program Courses Are Offered. The College Board sponsors the APP by offering college-level courses for high-ability students. If students perform well on the APP exams, it may enable them to either waive entry-level courses in college or actually earn college credit. The existence of APP courses can provide a continuing academic challenge for high school seniors. Note whether the school offers honors courses in addition to or instead of the APP courses.

SUPPORT FOR LEARNING

The areas covered in this section include:

Instructional resources (textbooks, science laboratory equipment, athletic equipment)

Technology resources (e.g., number of students/computer)

Counselor-student ratio

Aide-to-teacher ratio

Instructional/classroom resources may be indicated in a breakdown of expenditures at the website created by the state's department of education. Be alert to this particular expenditure that may affect the currency of textbooks, the sophistication of the science equipment, appropriate athletic equipment, or resources for the School Library Media Center. In Case Study 1 we noted that the expenditures had been low, but that there was a dramatic trend to improve this funding. Technology is an expensive resource that needs to be continually upgraded. In the next chapter, in the section "Richness of the Curriculum," we discuss recommended resources needed to support the academic subjects.

There are certainly disturbing differences in resources available to students in different states within the United States, as evidenced poignantly by Jonathan Kozol in *Savage Inequalities*. When on-site, it will be important to observe how a school is incorporating the resources it has within the learning environment. Have the teachers received appropriate training in the use of technological resources, for example?

Number of Students/Computer. Progress has been made in public school internet connectivity since 1994 when the federal government committed itself to assisting schools in this effort. Schools are also attempting to have every instructional room (e.g., every classroom, computer lab, and library/media center) connected to the internet. As of the fall of 1998, there were, on average, six students per instructional computer and twelve students per instructional computer with internet access (*Internet access in public schools and classrooms: 1994–98*).

Counselor–Student Ratio. The primary purpose of a school counselor is for academic and career guidance. Meeting with a counselor regularly will ensure that the student makes the appropriate curricular choices. The opportunity for proper guidance to take place is greater, of course, when there is an appropriate number of counselors available. The ratio recommended by the American School Counselor Association for all levels is: 1:250.

Aide-to-Teacher Ratio. Teaching is facilitated by the presence of aides and/or learning specialists (e.g., special education teachers) within the classroom. As noted in Case Study 1, a school that is intent upon the academic success of each of its students can be considerably benefited by the support offered by these specialists. In addition, structured study halls conducted by teachers and special education teachers offer further support to students.

STUDENT LIFE

Information about *cocurricular activities* of the school will provide an idea of the involvement and sense of ownership that students have of their school. These activities depend upon a mutual involvement of teachers and students so the number and range of activities can indicate the level of school community participation. Chapter 3 lists several possibilities for cocurricular activities and the case studies that follow indicate the wide range of offerings among schools.

A student newspaper and a student-prepared yearbook provide snapshots of the school community from the students' point of view. In Case Study 3 we noted that the student newspaper is available electronically via the school's website. The school's website can reflect other student input as well. In Case Study 1, the website is updated daily by students with, among other information, a photograph. The photograph may advertise a student art exhibit, a student-sponsored contest, or an upcoming event. Ask to have examples not available via the website sent to you or request them on-site.

Dropout Rate. The dropout status is defined as young adults (ages sixteen to twenty-four year olds) who are "not enrolled in a high school program and [have] not completed high school" (*Dropout rate*). The dropout rate as of October 1998 was 11.8 percent (*Dropout rate*), a consistent percentage over the last ten years. This is cause for concern because there is an increasing demand for a skilled labor force, making a high school education more essential. Reasons for dropping out may include academic dissatisfaction, pregnancy, or a record of suspensions.

Dropout rates may be reported differently. The following definitions indicate three different types of dropout rates.

Event rates "describe the proportion of students who leave school each year without completing a high school program. This annual measure of recent dropout occurrence provides important information about how effective educators are in keeping students enrolled in school" (*Dropout rate*). The event dropout rate as of October 1998 was 4.8 percent (*Dropout rate*).

Status rates "provide cumulative data on dropouts among all young adults within a specified age range. Status rates are higher than event rates because they include all dropouts ages sixteen through twenty-four, regardless of when they last attended school. Since status rates reveal the extent of the dropout problem in the population, these rates also can be used to estimate the need for further education and training designed to help dropouts participate fully in the economy and life of the nation" (*Dropout rate*).

Cohort rates "measure what happens to a group of students over a period of time. These rates are based on repeated measures of a cohort of students with shared experiences and reveal how many students starting in a specific grade drop out over time" (*Dropout rate*).

PARENT/COMMUNITY RELATIONS

Data may not be readily available for this category and this may be an area you choose to investigate further on-site. We learned about this area prior to the visit from sources such as the school's website, the course guides/program planning guide/curriculum offerings and proficiencies, the student/parent handbook, the student information booklet. These sources indicated to us the degree to which parents were invited to be a part of the school community and the expectation level that the school had of the parents.

CONCLUSION

Once the data review process has been completed, you will be in a position to list your questions in preparation for the on-site visit. The following chapter will provide further recommendations for the on-site evaluation.

REFERENCES

Baker, E. L. (1988). Can we fairly measure the quality of education? *NEA Today, 6* (6), 9–14.

Bobbitt, S., Quinn, P., & Dabbs, P. (1992). *Filling the gaps: An overview of data on education in grades K through 12.* Washington, DC: U.S. Department of Education, Office of Educational Research and Improvement, National Center for Education Statistics.

Derived information related to groups of students. National Center for Education Statistics [Online]. Available: Http://nces.ed.gov/pubs2000/studenthb/append_D.asp [June 10, 2000].

Dropout rate. (2000). National Center for Education Statistics [Online]. Available: Http://nces.ed.gov/ssbr/pages/dropout.asp [June 10, 2000].

Gerald, D. E. & Hussar, W. J. (1998). *Projections of education statistics to 2008.* Washington, DC: National Center for Education Statistics.

Internet access in public schools and classrooms: 1994–98. (February 1999). National Center for Education Statistics [Online]. Available: Http://nces.ed.gov/pubs99/1999017.html [June 10, 2000].

Kozol, J. (1991). *Savage inequalities: Children in America's schools.* New York: Crown Publishers.

Position statement on appropriate staffing for school library media centers. (2000). American Association of School Librarians, American Library Association [Online]. Available: Http://www.ala.org/aasl/positions/ps_schoolmedia.html [June 8, 2000].

Snyder, T. D. & Hoffman, C. M. (1998). *State comparisons of education statistics: 1969–70 to 1996–97.* Washington, DC: U.S. Department of Education, Office of Educational Research and Improvement, National Center for Education Statistics.

CHAPTER 3

A Guide to On-Site School Evaluation

Each person brings the personal experience of being educated—both positive and negative—to the examination of a school. When one remembers a rich learning experience, it is most likely the teacher who is remembered first, as it should be. The teacher knew how to make a connection with the student, how to make the learning experience come alive.

Yet the remembered teacher and the many like her or him do not live in isolation. They reside within a carefully created educational community and it is the job of the teacher to understand and respond to the individuals within that community and the larger community that embraces the school. When approaching a school, bring an understanding of the surrounding community with you, and then you will understand the purpose of the school. In Chapter 1 we discussed the historical background of education within the United States. The connections between the community's educational purpose and the greater national educational purpose should be evident.

On entering the school, observe both the physical environment and all who are working within it. The school will be working in association with the community to ensure that a safe and orderly environment for learning exists. The school is an integral part of the community and there should be evidence of collective support for the school's mission.

National studies mentioned in Appendix B (e.g., SASS) have collected data that provide an indication of school climate. Bobbitt, Quinn, and Dabbs (1992, p. 45) conclude that "it is clear from the data now available that student attitudes are directly affected by school climate and vice versa." Some of the data referred to includes: school problems, the level of academic challenge, and involvement by teachers and counselors. The students in particular can affect the climate by their attentiveness, level of preparation, boredom, absenteeism, and disruptiveness. A true understanding of the school's climate can only come from an on-site visit. The following recommendations have been drawn from the best of the effective education literature.

Upon entering the school, you might observe or ask:

- What is the school telling you about itself when you enter? Do you experience a positive school climate? Observe the bulletin boards (i.e., are they instructional) and displays of awards (i.e., are they for academic achievements, athletic achievements, celebrating the success of students and teachers).

- Note the attitude on the part of those who greet you (students, staff, teachers). Do you feel welcome? Is there evidence of a close-knit feeling and sense of loyalty to the school among the members of the school community?

- Is the building clean and well maintained?

- What is distinctive about the school?

- There should be evidence of open communication (both oral and written) and a sharing of information on the part of all members of the school community.

ORGANIZATIONAL AND ADMINISTRATIVE VITALITY/EFFECTIVENESS

Ask to tour the school with the principal or an individual designated by the principal and observe the interpersonal relationships among the staff and students. Respect for the principal is essential if that individual is to be effective in leading the school. A positive school climate should be evident as well as mutual respect between the administration and the school community.

When you are evaluating the organizational and administrative vitality/effectiveness of the school, you might observe or ask:

- How does the principal communicate a vision of the school's/district's mission?

- How does the principal communicate his or her educational values?

- Ask how the principal leads the process for school improvement and request evidence of this. For example, how are annual achievement test results, policies, curricula, and reports used in improvement plans? What are examples of incentives for learning?

- How does the principal monitor student progress?

- Ask about the curriculum and any new instructional programs. Familiarize yourself with Chapter 1 before your visit so that you can assess both the principal's knowledge of the instructional program and the program's currency. Even though you will be examining these with other school staff, it is important to find out how the principal responds. A more detailed guide to curriculum evaluation is given in the section "Richness of the Curriculum," which follows within this chapter.

- How does the principal evaluate the staff? What are the procedures for evaluation? Is constructive feedback given on a regular basis? Is the evaluation directly related to the teaching and learning process?
- Is classroom observation frequent?
- Does the principal consistently and clearly communicate high expectations for the teachers and students? Watch for evidence of communication (both oral and written) from the principal to staff, students, parents and the greater community.*
- Is the principal a strong decision-maker?*
- What evidence do you see of the principal's ability to plan and organize?*
- How does the principal both promote and provide staff development activities?*
- How does the principal supervise the teaching process?
- Is he or she capable of problem analysis?
- Does the principal demonstrate good judgment?
- Does he or she have a high tolerance for stress?
- Ask about faculty meetings and the subjects that are frequently discussed. Instructional issues should be a focus at these meetings.
- Ask for specific examples of ways that the principal protects time for teachers and students to stay on the task of learning. For example, are teachers involved with activities, such as recess duty, which take away from time that could be spent using their skills to better advantage? Teachers need time for planning. Is adequate time available for this process? Interruptions during instructional time should be kept to a minimum.
- Ask if block schedules are used. With this type of scheduling, three or four classes might meet for longer periods on alternate days. Some educators favor this schedule, which can promote in-depth study.
- Is the principal a subject specialist?
- Ask about the continued personal professional development of the principal.
- Ask the principal to describe new initiatives that the school has undertaken.
- Ask about ways that the school has renewed itself recently.
- What is the length of stay of the last three principals? Be aware of frequent administrative turnover.
- What methods does the school and the surrounding community use to ensure a safe and orderly environment for learning?
- Ask to see the school's code of conduct. Who created the code? How are appropriate behaviors (i.e., respect), attitudes, and beliefs modeled? Are there rewards for good citizenship? Are the consequences for breaking rules clearly articulated and what are the consequences if the code is violated? Is there a consistency in this area? Ask for examples of specific disciplinary measures.
- Ask if there has been a recent evaluation of the school.

---

* indicates that this characteristic is frequently mentioned in reference to effective school leadership.

THE INSTRUCTIONAL ENVIRONMENT (TEACHERS AND LEARNERS)

Ask to observe several classroom experiences. To be prepared for the classroom observations review the discussion of teaching styles and current educational trends in high school education in Chapter 1. Expect to observe several different learning environments, from the "traditional" lecture style of teaching and learning to "guide by the side" teaching and learning, with an encouragement for discussion in either case. Conceptual learning, rather than rote learning, should be evident. The schools that we visited for the case studies preferred that classroom observations be brief. We understand that it is difficult to assess an entire year of the teaching–learning experience from a few classroom observations. Many of the following recommendations would require a longer observation period, but we hesitate to omit them because your on-site visit may provide an opportunity for these observations to occur. Understanding the teaching–learning process is equally as important as measuring the outcomes of that process. A universally accepted system for measuring the effectiveness of a teacher has yet to be agreed on. In an attempt to assist you with enough insight into the instructional environment we offer the following suggestions.

The Teacher

When you are evaluating teaching, you might observe or ask:

- Watch for evidence that the teacher has made a connection with and understands the community she or he is serving.
- Ask about the teachers' professional development in their subject areas. Ask if any of the teachers participate in national or state professional organizations dedicated to the subject they are teaching. Ask if any teachers have received awards or recognition for excellence in their subject areas.
- Is the classroom atmosphere positive, challenging, and inspirational?
- Do the teachers enforce the rules of the school within the classroom? Is the teacher consistent in this area?
- Observe the interaction between teacher and student. Does the teacher communicate respect toward the students?
- How effectively does the teacher communicate the content to the students? Note content-related interaction taking place between the teacher and the students.
- Observe the nature of the questions the teacher is asking. Questions should require an answer that demonstrates analysis, synthesis, or evaluation of the information by the student.
- What encouragement do you see for creative thinking by the students?
- How well organized is the instruction session? Do you have a sense of the teacher's objectives? Has sufficient time been allowed for the amount of material to be cov-

ered? Are there any supplementary materials and are they sufficient and appropriate? Is the use of any type of equipment incorporated into the instruction session; how effective is this?

- Is there a sense of order to the classroom and the learning process taking place?

- Consider the appropriateness of the assignments being given.

- Watch for evidence of clarity when instructions and goals are given.

- Are interruptions during instructional time kept to a minimum?

- Is the teacher able to maintain an orientation toward the task at hand, with a focus on completing an activity?

- Are the instructional methods varied? (You should observe different methods used either in different classrooms and/or by one teacher.)

- Is the teacher respectful of the learning differences of the students? What are examples of classroom strategies that ensure successful learning for all students, including those with learning differences, different learning styles, and "multiple intelligences"? (Note examples that take place within the classroom itself rather than specifically designed programs that would remove the students from the classroom.)

- Note the teacher's awareness of diversity within the classroom. How does the teacher respond to differences in the students' interests and backgrounds?

- How are expectations for academic performance and behavior articulated to the students? Watch for behaviors that demonstrate that the teacher has high academic and behavioral expectations of the students.

- Note the classroom management skills of the teacher.

- What evaluation methods are used to ensure that learning is taking place? Are there several types of evaluation incorporated?

- What evidence do you see of creativity and innovation? Watch for this both from the teacher and within the classroom environment created by the teacher.

- Note examples of teachers modeling appropriate behaviors and attitudes.

- Are you aware of the teacher's intellectual curiosity?

- Do you sense that the teacher is a person who enjoys learning?

- Do you sense that the teacher enjoys what he or she is doing?

- How are the teachers encouraged by the school district to take advantage of professional development opportunities to keep abreast of current developments in education (e.g., do funds exist for this purpose)? What ongoing opportunities does the district itself make available to its teachers in the form of in-service education and other opportunities? Are there requirements for professional development and research by the teachers? In the section "Richness of the Curriculum," which follows, descriptions are given of rapidly changing curriculum needs. Curriculum development requires continuous learning on the part of teachers and sufficient time must be allotted for this process. Questions to ask about the financial support for professional development are given under the section "Support for Learning," which follows within this chapter. Ask if any of the following opportunities exist or are being taken advantage of:

Inservice days for staff development on the school calendar

Release time for observing other teachers

Courses offered by the school district after school or during the summer

Workshops for curriculum writing and development

Encouragement to be involved in state and regional training programs, summer institutes, and university courses

Access to subject specialists or consultants

- Ask what opportunities teachers have to learn from each other.
- How are new teachers trained?
- Ask about the teachers' involvement in schoolwide decision-making activities. Do the teachers make decisions about money allocations?
- Note the dedication level of the teachers by any unique involvement or contributions being made by members of the teaching community (this may be evidenced by a special program currently being promoted, e.g., an environmental project).
- Ask the number of years that the teachers in the school have been teaching, the number of years they have been teaching in the district, and the number of years they have been teaching in the building. Watch for stability within a school.

The Learner

Learning is hard work; there should be evidence of rigor. The students are being prepared for productive work, economic responsibility, and continued learning beyond high school. The curriculum must prepare students for a complex, multicultural society.

When you are evaluating the learner's experience, you might observe or ask:

- Be aware of opportunities for the students to experience different learning environments (e.g., working in small groups, working independently, receiving individual attention from the teacher, discussion).
- How are students encouraged to take responsibility for their own learning (i.e., to set goals; determine consequences; to select and complete tasks)?
- Note ways that the students support each other in the learning process.
- Look for ways in which the students seek information and additional resources for continued learning.
- Does the curriculum encourage students to work beyond the required expectations?
- Do the students "get by" with minimal effort?
- How is the learner made responsible for completing a task effectively? Is self-evaluation part of the process?
- How are the students rewarded for their efforts in order to encourage them to appreciate the success of their efforts?
- Note the affective behaviors of the students (interest, attitude, intrinsic motivation, self-concept).
- What evidence do you see of hard work and persistence on the part of the students?

- How does the curriculum encourage the development of the individual in terms of acceptance of responsibility and encouragement of free expression?
- What are examples that you see of cooperative learning among the students?
- What activities promote peer support for learning?
- How are the students learning problem-solving skills, communication skills, and teamwork skills?
- How are the students learning to make decisions and choices?
- How are students participating in curriculum design?

RICHNESS OF THE CURRICULUM

As discussed in Chapter 1, in today's schools there is a shift away from rote memorization and sequential learning of basic skills toward a focus on the development of thinking skills, discovering patterns and relationships, and reflecting.

The following academic subjects will be the focus of this section: language arts, mathematics, social studies, science, the arts, and information literacy. We will also discuss moral education, foreign languages, English as a second language, and transition to work programs. For examples that describe how particular schools are demonstrating excellence in these subject areas, we encourage the reader to consult the case studies in Chapter 4 and sources such as *The Nation's Best Schools* (Ogden & Germinario, 1995).

In several of the subject areas we refer to standards prepared by national organizations. These standards were prepared with substantial contributions from classroom teachers, parents, legislators, administrators, researchers, and policy analysts. They are intended to provide criteria by which local and state education systems develop their own individual curriculum. Each of the standards recognizes the need to adequately prepare students for further education and for "socialization into a complex society" (Goodlad, 1984, p. 37). Literacy in each of the curriculum areas is a necessity for all students and the standards recommended assume equitable opportunity for all students. In the case studies we refer to these standards when assessing the curriculum from the schools' course guides. It is possible to assess whether the curriculum is meeting the basic outline of the standards. The details, of course, can only be determined by experiencing the teaching–learning situation and reviewing the complete curriculum guides. These overviews of the standards, then, will serve as a guide for an introductory assessment of the curriculum. State standards, developed in response to the national standards, may also be referred to in the school's course guide, as we found in Case Study 3.

Language Arts

The National Council of Teachers of English (NCTE) has published the following list of standards for the English language arts. For information about these standards, refer to *http://ncte.org/standards/thelist.html*.

NCTE recommends that the standards be considered as a whole and not as distinct or separable:

1. Students read a wide range of print and nonprint texts to build an understanding of texts, of themselves, and of the cultures of the United States and the world; to acquire new information; to respond to the needs and demands of society and the workplace; and for personal fulfillment. Among these texts are fiction and nonfiction, classic and contemporary works.

2. Students read a wide range of literature from many periods in many genres to build an understanding of the many dimensions (e.g., philosophical, ethical, aesthetic) of human experience.

3. Students apply a wide range of strategies to comprehend, interpret, evaluate, and appreciate texts. They draw on their prior experience, their interactions with other readers and writers, their knowledge of word meaning and of other texts, their word identification strategies, and their understanding of textual features (e.g., sound-letter correspondence, sentence structure, context, graphics).

4. Students adjust their use of spoken, written, and visual language (e.g., conventions, style, vocabulary) to communicate effectively with a variety of audiences and for different purposes.

5. Students employ a wide range of strategies as they write and use different writing process elements appropriately to communicate with different audiences for a variety of purposes.

6. Students apply knowledge of language structure, language conventions (e.g., spelling and punctuation), media techniques, figurative language, and genre to create, critique, and discuss print and nonprint texts.

7. Students conduct research on issues and interests by generating ideas and questions, and by posing problems. They gather, evaluate, and synthesize data from a variety of sources (e.g., print and nonprint texts, artifacts, people) to communicate their discoveries in ways that suit their purpose and audience.

8. Students use a variety of technological and information resources (e.g., libraries, databases, computer networks, video) to gather and synthesize information and to create and communicate knowledge.

9. Students develop an understanding of and respect for diversity in language use, patterns, and dialects across cultures, ethnic groups, geographic regions, and social roles.

10. Students whose first language is not English make use of their first language to develop competency in the English language arts and to develop understanding of content across the curriculum

11. Students participate as knowledgeable, reflective, creative, and critical members of a variety of literacy communities.

12. Students use spoken, written, and visual language to accomplish their own purposes (e.g., for learning, enjoyment, persuasion, and the exchange of information).

Watch for learning opportunities developed especially for the school's curriculum that will assist students in making connections among reading, writing, and oral language.

When you are evaluating the language arts curriculum *of the school, you might observe or ask:*

- Are reading selections literature based or are students taught literature fragments or taught from condensed versions?

- Are writing skills taught for several purposes (e.g., technical writing, or writing to inform audiences, persuade, narrate, describe, entertain, or communicate via e-mail)?

- Is sufficient time allotted for opportunities to make connections among writing, reading, speaking, and listening?

- How is language arts integrated with other areas of the curriculum? Ask if the school has programs such as Writing Across the Curriculum. Is literature taught in relation to history, science, or the arts?

- How are students encouraged to reflect on what they're reading?

- Are the students writing every day?

- What formal opportunities exist for speaking and listening (e.g., panel discussions)?

Mathematics

For a thorough discussion of the recommended mathematical standards published by the National Council of Teachers of Mathematics (NCTM) we refer the reader to the *Principles and Standards for School Mathematics* at *http://www.nctm.org/standards*. The standards for grades 9 to 12 are at: *http://standards.nctm.org/protoFINAL/chapter7/introduction.html*.

All students require adequate preparation for the information society and for the impact of technology on our society. As with each curriculum area, there is an emphasis in the mathematics standards on using knowledge. Knowledge of mathematics is demonstrated through reasoning and problem-solving skills. Although the career goals of students will determine their specific mathematics curriculum, NCTM recommends the following for all high school students:

A. Mathematical study in each of the four years of high school
B. Knowledge and ability in each of the following areas (individual standards exist for each):

  1. Number and operations
  2. Algebra
  3. Geometry
  4. Measurement
  5. Data analysis and probability

6. Problem solving
7. Reasoning and proof
8. Communication
9. Connections
10. Representation

There is an emphasis within these standards on "fundamental concepts, thinking and reasoning, modeling, and communicating" and the central theme of the standards is "connections" (*NCTM*).

When you are evaluating the mathematics curriculum *of the school, you might observe or ask:*

- In what ways is the school utilizing the NCTM standards in developing its curriculum?
- Does the school incorporate any particular programs into its mathematics curriculum such as Activities that Integrate Math and Science (AIMS)?
- Is there a math resource center staffed by a math teacher for all or part of the day?

Social Studies

The *Standards and Position Statements* of the National Council for the Social Studies (NCSS) appear at *http://www.ncss.org/standards/home.html.* These standards are based on ten thematic strands, further described at the above website.

1. *Culture.* As students progress through high school, they can understand and use complex cultural concepts such as adaptation, assimilation, acculturation, diffusion, and dissonance drawn from anthropology, sociology, and other disciplines to explain how culture and cultural systems function. . . .
2. *Time, Continuity, and Change.* High school students engage in more sophisticated analysis and reconstruction of the past, examining its relationship to the present and extrapolating into the future. They integrate individual stories about people, events, and situations to form a more holistic conception, in which continuity and change are linked in time and across cultures. Students also learn to draw on their knowledge of history to make informed choices and decisions in the present. . . .
3. *People, Places, and Environments.* Students in high school are able to apply geographic understanding across a broad range of fields, including the fine arts, sciences, and humanities. Geographic concepts become central to learners' comprehension of global connections as they expand their knowledge of diverse cultures, both historical and contemporary. The importance of core geographic themes to public policy is recognized and should be explored as students address issues of domestic and international significance. . . .
4. *Individual Development and Identity.* At the high school level, students need to encounter multiple opportunities to examine contemporary patterns of human behavior, using methods from the behavioral sciences to apply core concepts drawn

from psychology, social psychology, sociology, and anthropology as they apply to individuals, societies, and cultures. . . .

5. *Individuals, Groups, and Institutions.* High school students must understand the paradigms and traditions that undergird social and political institutions. They should be provided opportunities to examine, use, and add to the body of knowledge related to the behavioral sciences and social theory as it relates to the ways people and groups organize themselves around common needs, beliefs, and interests. . . .

6. *Power, Authority, and Governance.* High school students develop their abilities in the use of abstract principles. They study the various systems that have been developed over the centuries to allocate and employ power and authority in the governing process. At every level, learners should have opportunities to apply their knowledge and skills to and participate in the workings of the various levels of power, authority, and governance. . . .

7. *Production, Distribution, and Consumption.* High school students develop economic perspectives and deeper understanding of key economic concepts and processes through systematic study of a range of economic and sociopolitical systems, with particular emphasis on the examination of domestic and global economic policy options related to matters such as health care, resource use, unemployment, and trade. . . .

8. *Science, Technology, and Society.* As they move from the middle grades to high school, students will need to think more deeply about how we can manage technology so that we control it rather than the other way around. There should be opportunities to confront such issues as the consequences of using robots to produce goods, the protection of privacy in the age of computers and electronic surveillance, and the opportunities and challenges of genetic engineering, test-tube life, and medical technology with all their implications for longevity and quality of life and religious beliefs. . . .

9. *Global Connections.* At the high school level, students are able to think systematically about personal, national, and global decisions, interactions, and consequences, including addressing critical issues such as peace, human rights, trade, and global ecology. . . .

10. *Civic Ideals and Practices.* High school students increasingly recognize the rights and responsibilities of citizens in identifying societal needs, setting directions for public policies, and working to support both individual dignity and the common good. They learn by experience how to participate in community service and political activities and how to use democratic process to influence public policy. (*Standards and Position Statements*)

When you are evaluating the social studies curriculum *of the school, you might observe or ask:*

- What does the school base its social studies curriculum on and if the standards mentioned above are integral to the school's development of its social studies curriculum?

- Do students in their study of social studies

    Use multiple sources
    Use original documents
    Use historical narratives
    Write essays
    Use technology
    Research information
    Produce individual and group research papers
    Evaluate and critique sources
    Draw conclusions
    Debate
    Construct logical arguments

- Is the literature component of the language arts curriculum coordinated with the social studies curriculum so that fiction and nonfiction selections related to history are taught?

- Are joint social studies/English research and writing experiences offered?

- Is science integrated with social studies?

- Are both American history and world history required?

- Are physical and cultural geography integrated into the history courses?

- Do students study social studies for four or more years (from middle school through high school)?

- Are competitive experiences offered such as: Mock Trial, We the People . . . The Citizen and the Constitution competition, and Model UN?

Science

The National Research Council (NRC), the principal operating agency of the National Academy of Sciences and the National Academy of Engineering, coordinated the development of the National Science Education Standards (NSES) in 1995. The project was funded by the National Science Foundation, U.S. Department of Education, National Aeronautics and Space Administration, and National Institutes of Health. For more information about these standards, see *http:// books.nap.edu/ html/nses*.

The outline prepared by the NRC of the Science Content Standards for grades 9 to 12 follows.

Science as Inquiry
CONTENT STANDARD A: As a result of activities in grades 9–12, all students should develop

- Abilities necessary to do scientific inquiry

- Understandings about scientific inquiry . . .

Physical Science

CONTENT STANDARD B: As a result of their activities in grades 9–12, all students should develop an understanding of

- Structure of atoms
- Structure and properties of matter
- Chemical reactions
- Motions and forces
- Conservation of energy and increase in disorder
- Interactions of energy and matter . . .

Life Science

CONTENT STANDARD C: As a result of their activities in grades 9–12, all students should develop an understanding of

- The cell
- Molecular basis of heredity
- Biological evolution
- Interdependence of organisms
- Matter, energy, and organization in living systems
- Behavior of organisms . . .

Earth and Space Science

CONTENT STANDARD D: As a result of their activities in grades 9–12, all students should develop an understanding of

- Energy in the earth system
- Geochemical cycles
- Origin and evolution of the earth system
- Origin and evolution of the universe . . .

Science and Technology

CONTENT STANDARD E: As a result of activities in grades 9–12, all students should develop

- Abilities of technological design
- Understandings about science and technology . . .

Science in Personal and Social Perspectives

CONTENT STANDARD F: As a result of activities in grades 9–12, all students should develop an understanding of

- Personal and community health
- Population growth
- Natural resources
- Environmental quality
- Natural and human-induced hazards
- Science and technology in local, national, and global challenges . . .

History and Nature of Science

CONTENT STANDARD G: As a result of activities in grades 9–12, all students should develop an understanding of

- Science as a human endeavor
- Nature of scientific knowledge
- Historical perspectives . . .

Reprinted [and adapted] with permission from *National Science Education Standards*. Copyright 1996 by the National Academy of Sciences. Courtesy of the National Academy Press, Washington, DC.

When you are evaluating the science curriculum *of the school, you might observe or ask:*

- Is the curriculum thematically based (i.e., developed from programs such as Activities that Integrate Math and Science [AIMS])?
- Are the students:

    Actively engaged in doing science

    Observing, collecting, recording, and analyzing data

    Making hypotheses

    Communicating and supporting their findings

    Using technology to access resources

    Using computers to analyze data

    Taking field trips (day, overnight, and/or weeklong experiences)

    Communicating with local resource people (e.g., from industry, colleges, or museums)

    Integrating science with other areas of the curriculum such as Writing Across the Curriculum?

- Are cooperative learning groups used to model how scientists work?

The Arts

The National Standards for Arts Education (NSAE) were developed by the Consortium of National Arts Education Associations (American Alliance for Theatre & Education, Music Educators National Conference, National Art Education Association, and the National Dance Association) and published in 1994. A brief summary of the standards follows; for more information about the standards, consult *http://artsedge.kennedy-center.org/forms/arts1.html*.

Within the standards document, art is defined as "(1) creative works and the process of producing them, and (2) the whole body of work in the art forms that make up the entire human intellectual and cultural heritage." The arts refers to dance, music, theatre, and the visual arts. Among the benefits for a study of the arts as an integral portion of the educational experience are the development of:

- Understanding human experiences, both past and present;

- Learning to adapt to and respect others' (often very different) ways of thinking, working, and expressing themselves;
- Learning artistic modes of problem solving, which bring an array of expressive, analytical, and developmental tools to every human situation (this is why we speak, for example, of the "art" of teaching or the "art" of politics);
- Understanding the influences of the arts, for example, in their power to create and reflect cultures, in the impact of design on virtually all we use in daily life, and in the interdependence of work in the arts with the broader worlds of ideas and action;
- Making decisions in situations where there are no standard answers;
- Analyzing nonverbal communication and making informed judgments about cultural products and issues; and
- Communicating their thoughts and feelings in a variety of modes, giving them a vastly more powerful repertoire of self-expression.

Excerpted and adapted from *National Standards for Arts Education.* Copyright 1994 by Music Educators National Conference. Used by permission.

When you are evaluating the arts curriculum *of the school, you might observe or ask:*

- What is the specific curriculum? One approach used by many schools is Discipline-Based Arts Education (DBAE) that promotes student development in art history, criticism, production, and aesthetics.
- Is the school involved in any partnerships (e.g., ArtsEDGE, Arts Education Partnership, Research in Learning in Museums)? For more information about these partnerships see the National Endowment for the Arts NEA Partnerships website at *http://www.arts.endow.gov/partner/*.
- Are there choral groups?
- Are there instrumental groups?

Information Literacy

The teaching of information literacy is frequently the responsibility of the School Library Media Center (SLMC) Specialist. This specialist is a partner with the classroom teachers in curriculum design and a proponent of resource-based learning. The position statement of the American Association of School Librarians (AASL) proposes that the following elements be the basis of an information literacy curriculum:

1. Defining the need for information
2. Initiating the search strategy
3. Locating the resources
4. Assessing and comprehending the information
5. Interpreting the information
6. Communicating the information
7. Evaluating the product and process (*Information Literacy*)

(Reprinted with permission from AASL, ALA, and Wisconsin Educational Media Association.)

For details about each of these elements, please refer to the AASL Position Statement on Information Literacy at *http://www.ala.org/aasl/positions/ps_infolit.html*.

Technology is expensive and in the following suggested questions it is expected that the average high school will not have access to all the recommended resources. Ask about the school's plans and process for obtaining technology and how the school's budget reflects the school's commitment to information literacy.

When you are evaluating the information literacy *component of the curriculum your observations will include the school library media center. You might observe or ask*:

- Is there an individual assigned to facilitate the information literacy component of the curriculum? This person may be the school library media center specialist.

- Is there at least one certificated library media specialist working full-time in the school library media center? In addition, AASL recommends at least one full-time technical assistant or clerk for each library media specialist.

- Is there a school district library media director?

- What are specific examples of ways in which the information literacy curriculum is meeting the basic elements recommended by AASL?

- Does the school provide a sufficient quantity and quality of the following to meet the needs of the student body:

    Up-to-date traditional print materials, including books, charts, magazines, and prints. Keep in mind that many valuable resources are only available in the print (paper) form.

    Computers

    CD-ROMs that provide access to data

    Scientific and graphing calculators

    Satellite dishes

    Cable television

    Information retrieval services

    Internet access

    Software, laser discs, video- and audiotapes

    Televisions

    Camcorders

    Fax machines

- What is the access to the above resources? All students should have equal access. This can be done by providing the access within the school day, offering after-school access, and loaning resources to students.

- Is the school library media center the central hub for access to and distribution of technology?

- Are there one or more labs available for word processing, publishing, or information access?

- Does the school have any portable computers? Are any of these available to be loaned to students after school hours?

- Do classrooms have mini-labs composed of five to seven computers?

- Is there a multimedia teaching station in each classroom?

- Are all computers networked to a server in the school library media center or connected to remote sites?

- Is there electronic access throughout the school and remotely to the catalog of the collections of the school library media center?

- What educational software is available and how it is integrated into the curriculum?

Foreign Language

Adequate preparation for communicating within a global society requires foreign language preparation. The *Standards for Foreign Language Learning in the 21st Century*, published by the National Standards in Foreign Language Education Project, appear at: *http://www.actfl.org/htdocs/standards/standards.htm*. These standards are governed by the following statement of philosophy:

Language and communication are at the heart of the human experience. The United States must educate students who are linguistically and culturally equipped to communicate successfully in a pluralistic American society and abroad. This imperative envisions a future in which ALL students will develop and maintain proficiency in English and at least one other language, modern or classical. Children who come to school from non-English backgrounds should also have opportunities to develop further proficiencies in their first language. (*Standards for Foreign Language Learning*)

The standards cover the following areas:

Communication

Communicate in Languages Other Than English

Standard 1.1: Students engage in conversations, provide and obtain information, express feelings and emotions, and exchange opinions.

Standard 1.2: Students understand and interpret written and spoken language on a variety of topics.

Standard 1.3: Students present information, concepts, and ideas to an audience of listeners or readers on a variety of topics.

Cultures

Gain Knowledge and Understanding of Other Cultures

Standard 2.1: Students demonstrate an understanding of the relationship between the practices and perspectives of the culture studied.

Standard 2.2: Students demonstrate an understanding of the relationship between the products and perspectives of the culture studied.

Connections
Connect with Other Disciplines and Acquire Information
Standard 3.1: Students reinforce and further their knowledge of other disciplines through the foreign language.
Standard 3.2: Students acquire information and recognize the distinctive viewpoints that are only available through the foreign language and its cultures.

Comparisons
Develop Insight into the Nature of Language and Culture
Standard 4.1: Students demonstrate understanding of the nature of language through comparisons of language studied and their own.
Standard 4.2: Students demonstrate understanding of the concept of culture through comparisons of the cultures studied and their own.

Communities
Participate in Multilingual Communities at Home and Around the World
Standard 5.1: Students use the language both within and beyond the school setting.
Standard 5.2: Students show evidence of becoming lifelong learners by using the language for personal enjoyment and enrichment.

(Reprinted with permission from National Standards in Foreign Language Education Project [1999]. *Standards for Foreign Language Learning in the 21st Century.* Yonkers, NY: National Standards in Foreign Language Education Project.)

When you are evaluating the foreign language curriculum *of the school, you might observe or ask:*

- Have the students in the district begun foreign language instruction at the elementary or middle school level?
- Is the school offering at least Spanish or French, and possibly German and Latin?

English as a Second Language (ESL)

The needs of the school population will determine the requirements for an ESL program. School districts vary in need from those with no non-English-speaking students to 80 percent of the student body with native languages other than English.

When you are evaluating the English as a second language curriculum *of the school, you might observe or ask:*

- Are all of the teachers in the school trained for instructing students with limited English proficiency?
- Is the support of peers who speak the student's native language available?
- Is there parental contact in the native language?
- Is bilingual tutoring available?
- Are there advisory groups for the ESL program?
- Are there any Saturday or summer programs available?

Transition to Work Programs

For those who do not immediately plan to continue with formal education beyond high school, transition to work programs prepare students for entry into the workforce while also requiring high academic expectations designed to prepare them for a postsecondary education. Vocational opportunities should exist that are geared to "developing readiness for productive work and economic responsibility" (Goodlad, 1984, p. 37).

When you are evaluating the transition to work program *of the school, you might observe or ask:*

- Is the program designed to coordinate with at least two years of postsecondary education?
- What careers are available for the students to experience? Is this done with mentorship programs, internships, and/or work–study programs?

Moral Education

Moral education has a long history. As we know from the common school movement, the teaching of universal principles was intended to bridge the gaps between differing morals and beliefs. Today our public school communities are increasingly pluralistic and there are conflicting views about what constitute universal moral values.

Educators have built on John Dewey's theory that the "proper way to resolve moral dilemmas in real life is to apply reason or intelligent thought" (ASCD Panel on Moral Education, 1988, p. 6). Educational settings have incorporated the values clarification approach, the values analysis approach, the psychological education program, and more, including current self-esteem programs.

Moral education is the shared responsibility of families, communities, religious communities, and schools. Some feel that moral education in schools is essential, for "at the heart of democracy is the morally mature citizen" (ASCD, p. 7). The ASCD Panel on Moral Education further states (ASCD, p. 5) that "to be moral means to *value* morality, to take moral obligations seriously. It means to be able to judge what is right but also to care deeply about doing it—and to possess the will, competence, and habits needed to translate moral judgment and feeling into effective moral action." Recognizing that the definition of moral maturity is one that is fluid and requires constant reexamination, the ASCD Panel on Moral Education has suggested the following six major defining characteristics of a morally mature person (ASCD, p. 5). The morally mature person habitually:

1. *Respects human dignity*, which includes
    Showing regard for the worth and rights of all persons
    Avoiding deception and dishonesty
    Promoting human equality

Respecting freedom of conscience

Working with people of different views

Refraining from prejudiced actions

2. *Cares about the welfare of others*, which includes

Recognizing interdependence among people

Caring for one's country

Seeking social justice

Taking pleasure in helping others

Working to help others reach moral maturity

3. *Integrates individual interests and social responsibilities*, which includes

Becoming involved in community life

Doing a fair share of community work

Displaying self-regarding and other-regarding moral virtues—self-control, diligence, fairness, kindness, honesty, civility—in everyday life

Fulfilling commitments

Developing self-esteem through relationships with others

4. *Demonstrates integrity*, which includes

Practicing diligence

Taking stands for moral principles

Displaying moral courage

Knowing when to compromise and when to confront

Accepting responsibility for one's choices

5. *Reflects on moral choices*, which includes

Recognizing the moral issues involved in a situation

Applying moral principles (such as the golden rule) when making moral judgments

Thinking about the consequences of decisions

Seeking to be informed about important moral issues in society and the world

6. *Seeks peaceful resolution of conflict*, which includes

Striving for the fair resolution of personal and social conflicts

Avoiding physical and verbal aggression

Listening carefully to others

Encouraging others to communicate

Working for peace

(ASCD Panel on Moral Education. Reprinted with permission from ASCD. All rights reserved.)

In general, the morally mature person understands moral principles and ac-
cepts responsibility for applying them.

When you are evaluating the moral education *of the school, you might observe
or ask:*

• What guiding principles does the school use for a values education or a moral education?

- How is the school incorporating a values education or moral education into its curriculum?

- How is the school assessing moral education?

When you are evaluating the overall curriculum of the school, you might further observe or ask:

- Is there a direct relationship between the curriculum and the school's mission?

- How is the school serving the varying educational needs of the population in the areas of: language literacy, advanced placements, learning disorders, emotional needs? Ask about these specific programs and the training of the teachers and counselors to serve these populations.

- Be alert to the complexity of the material being taught. Students should be facing complex problems in order to develop conceptual thinking skills.

- Is writing competency encouraged in all subject areas?

- Ask for examples of ways in which multiculturalism is encouraged within the curriculum.

- What are the minimal competencies required at each grade level?

- How does the school communicate its academic expectations to both students and parents?

- Observe the use of technology in the classroom. How is it integrated into the learning experience?

- How are internships, apprenticeships, and community service opportunities incorporated into the curriculum?

- Observe skills being taught that will enable students to continue their learning process beyond high school (e.g., study skills, organizational skills, time management, information-seeking skills).

- How does the school create connections for the students with learning places beyond the school such as libraries, museums, art galleries, colleges, and industry?

- Ask for evidence that the curriculum is equally challenging for both gifted and special needs students. Is the expectation for rigorous study in demanding subjects the same for all students?

- Does the school use a "tracking system"? If so, what benefits does the school see in this system and how does the system encourage equal education opportunities? "From a learning point of view, tracking has . . . been shown to be ineffective; however, while tracking is an undesirable practice, flexible groupings and cooperative groups have immediate benefits in terms of learning content and for learning to function as part of a team. In addition, honors level and advanced placement courses can provide opportunities for interested students to explore subjects at very high levels" (Ogden & Germinario, 1995, p. 199).

- How are the students being prepared in the personal area, "emphasizing the development of individual responsibility, talent, and free expression" (Goodlad, p. 37)?

- How are the measures of pupil achievement used as the basis to evaluate the curriculum? (More specific questions appear in the following section, "Academic Achievement.")

- What is the process and frequency for curriculum assessment and revision?

ACADEMIC ACHIEVEMENT

Students need to be assessed not only on knowledge gained but on the application or performance of that knowledge. Three traditional categories of assessment, some discussed in Chapter 1, are: (a) criterion-referenced, which compares the child's knowledge to what the school expected the child to learn; (b) norm-referenced, which compares the child's knowledge to that of other children; (c) child-referenced, which compares the child's knowledge after instruction to what he or she knew before (Oakes & Lipton, 1990, p. 130). Student achievement tests, discussed in more detail earlier, frequently serve as a prominent measure of the student's progress. "Standardized tests give the school system perspective about its relationship to the state, regional, or national picture. A few words of caution should be offered, however, about standardized tests: They should not be assumed to be so important that they alone determine the curriculum. If tests were to determine the curriculum, the program would lose the depth of richness it can enjoy with a creative teacher" (Johnson, 1991, p. 516). It is important to note the methods that a school uses to encourage academic achievement in addition to noting the achievement results.

When you are evaluating the academic achievement *of the school, you might observe or ask*:

- What types of assessment are used? Students should be assessed both on knowledge and performance. They should consistently be assessed on their abilities to:

    Read and interpret what they have read
    Retrieve and select information, analyze information, and evaluate information
    Organize their ideas
    Express their ideas both in verbal and written formats
    Ask questions

- Within each subject area are there multiple assessment techniques, including written, oral, process and performance/product formats (e.g., portfolio, research papers, multiple-choice exams, essays, oral reports, graphs, maps, debates, experiments, critique, etc.)? This allows an opportunity for corroboration of the performance results. There should be some measurement techniques that provide sufficient time for involved cognitive tasks.

- What does a sample report card look like? In addition to letter grades there should be some indication of what the student has actually learned. If this information is not given, ask how the school communicates that information to parents (e.g., open houses, back-to-school nights, regularly scheduled parent–teacher–student conferences, other written reports in addition to report cards) (Oakes & Lipton, 1990, p. 20).

- What efforts does a school make to keep students from falling behind? Ask about specific examples of support both within the school day and beyond.

- When the school recognizes a student's difficulties, how does it proactively treat them? What are examples of intervention strategies and how quickly were they implemented?

- Are the school's expectations for achievement the same for all students? Are the expectations realized?

- How are good efforts and productivity by both teachers and students rewarded? What kind of communications are made privately to students about their progress?

- Is there consistency across the program for frequent monitoring and assessing of student progress? How are expectations of students monitored, reviewed, and clarified?

- What are the school's expectations for college attendance? Does the school keep track of its students' post high school performance (e.g., percentage that complete college)?

- How are assessment results used? Note if there has been significant improvement or change over time. When achievement results are compared over time, which cohort groups are compared (e.g., socioeconomic status, ethnicity, achievement level)? Does the performance improve within these groups?

With each of the above observations be alert to the community's demographics and whether the school is focusing on the entire community. Note the time period covered and ask what the school has learned from the results and what their response has been.

Note: How are achievement results compared internally (within the school)? (This information may appear on the school's website.) How are achievement results compared externally (with district and national results)? (This information may also appear on the school's website.)

SUPPORT FOR LEARNING

This section emphasizes the financial assistance given to learning support, which includes resources necessary for the curriculum areas and professional development opportunities. The school library media center is discussed in the earlier section "Richness of the Curriculum" and serves as a vital support for each curriculum area.

When you are evaluating the support for learning *of the school, you might observe or ask:*

- How are the services of the guidance counselors utilized most effectively to assist students with their career decisions? Are any career workshops provided?

- What ways do guidance counselors contribute to the emotional health of the organization (e.g., are workshops given for students, teachers, and parents to address current needs of the school community)? Are the counselors proactive? How do they respond to problems?

- Is there financial support for the continuing education of teachers? Are any of the following resources used to support the costs of substitute teachers for release time, travel expenses, summer workshop pay for teachers, registration fees, professional literature, or training consultants' fees:

    District funds

    Business partners (may provide technical assistance and/or financial resources)

    University partners (may provide technical assistance and training)

    Networks (may provide financial resources and/or expertise)

    Special fund-raising

    Foundations

    Release time to observe instruction

    PTAs or PTOs

- In regard to the social studies curriculum, ask about the following resources:

    Sufficient up-to-date maps and globes

    Fiction and nonfiction books available either in class collections or through the school library media center

    News sources

    General materials for projects

    Current textbooks

    Access to remote databases

- In regard to the science curriculum, ask about the following resources:

    Measuring devices

    Stereo microscopes

    Electronic meters

    Still and video cameras

    Calculators

    Computers

    Animals

    Garden plots

    Natural areas for study

- In regard to the arts curriculum, ask about the following resources:

    Live performances at the school

    Field trips to museums and performances

    Musical instruments for those students who cannot afford to purchase their own

- Ask about funding to support students for:

    Visits to museums, science centers, and historical sites, or overnight trips for the in-depth study of science

    Travel funds for competitions

    Travel funds for scientific study of the existing environment within the community or to nearby areas

STUDENT LIFE

Ask if a recent student satisfaction survey has been conducted and how the school responded to the results.

When you are evaluating the student life *of the school, you might observe or ask:*

- What cocurricular activities are there? These may include community service opportunities in addition to those directly linked to the curriculum. There should be a wide variety to appeal to the needs of all students.
- The following is a checklist of several types of cocurricular activities offered in high schools. The selection of activities is based on student need and availability of faculty to supervise the activity. However, be alert to multiple opportunities afforded to the student.

    School publications
        School newspaper
        Literary magazine
        Yearbook
    Academic clubs
        Student government
        Foreign language
        Gifted and talented
        Debating team / mock trial
        Public speaking / forensics
        Science
        Computer
        Mathematics
    Fine arts programs
        Drama
        Audiovisual / Media
        Art
        Photography
        Orchestra
        Marching band
    Other cocurricular programs
        Environmental club
        Students Against Drunk Driving (SADD)
        Students Against Drug Abuse (SADA)
        Cheerleaders
        Ski club
        Driver's education (behind the wheel)

- Athletic teams that may exist at the high school level include the following:

    Football
    Basketball

Wrestling
Soccer
Field hockey
Lacrosse
Ice hockey
Skiing
Baseball
Softball
Tennis
Gymnastics
Swimming
Track & field / cross-country
Golf
Volleyball
Bowling
Fencing

PARENT/COMMUNITY RELATIONS

Your initial evaluation of the school began in Chapter 2 with an assessment of the community within which the school exists. Consider what you have learned about the surrounding community and the school community and now examine the ways in which the school directly interacts with the community. What are examples of community-building efforts between the school community and the surrounding community of parents, business persons, nonprofit institutions, and other community organizations (e.g., Kiwanis Club, Women's Club, public libraries, museums, music organizations)?

When you are evaluating the parent/community relations *of the school, you might observe or ask:*

- What specific policies and activities exist to promote parent/community member involvement in the schools?
- Are there established guidelines for parental/community member involvement?
- What role does the principal play in promoting involvement?
- How are parents and community groups invited to contribute to the success of the school? What are examples of parents and community members serving as partners, collaborators, problem-solvers, supporters, advisors, or co-decision-makers with the schools?
- What formal opportunities exist for parents/community members to share in governance and decision-making for the schools?
- How do the students know that the school and the surrounding community care about them?

- What are examples of support for the school by the surrounding community that demonstrate that the community is proud of the school and the performance of the students?
- How does the school create partnerships with all families in the school?
- How are parents informed when students need more support from the home or from outside the school to sustain an acceptable achievement level?
- Are communications with parents frequent?
- How are parent and community volunteers used within the classroom?
- What are examples of some of the recent accomplishments of the volunteer parent/community organization?
- What opportunities exist for formal interaction between school administrators, teachers, students, parents, and community members?
- What intergenerational activities take place between the school and the surrounding community?
- What formal opportunities are there for parents/community members to be involved in the curriculum development?
- What formal opportunities are there for parents/community members to assess their schools?
- Do speakers from the community visit the school frequently to reinforce the relationship between learning and the world of work?
- Are there any obstacles for parent or community member involvement? How have some of these obstacles been overcome?

CONCLUSION

We hope that when you have completed your on-site visit you will have a good understanding of the organization of the school community. There are many processes to observe in order to know if a school is effective for your child. The case studies that follow were instrumental in confirming for us the necessity of observing all elements of the school community in action. A positive balance in each of the categories will help you to know if the school is effective.

REFERENCES

ASCD Panel on Moral Education. (May 1988). Moral education in the life of the school. *Educational Leadership, 45* (9), 4–8. Reprinted with permission from the Association for Supervision and Curriculum Development (ASCD). All rights reserved.

Bobbitt, S., Quinn, P., & Dabbs, P. (1992). *Filling the gaps: An overview of data on education in grades K through 12.* Washington, DC: U.S. Department of Education, Office of Educational Research and Improvement, National Center for Education Statistics.

Goodlad, J. I. (1984). *A place called school.* New York: McGraw-Hill.

Information literacy: A position paper on information problem solving. American Association of School Librarians, American Library Association, Wisconsin Educational Media Association [Online]. Available: Http://www.ala.org/aasl/positions/ps_infolit.html [June 13, 2000]. Extracts reprinted with permission from AASL, ALA.

Johnson, J. A. et al. (Eds.). (1991). *Introduction to the foundations of education* (Annotated instructor's edition). Boston: Allyn and Bacon.

NCTM: Principles and standards for school mathematics. (2000). National Council of Teachers of Mathematics [Online]. Available: Http://www.nctm.org/standards [June 10, 2000].

National Council of Teachers of English: The list of standards for the English language arts. National Council of Teachers of English and the International Reading Association [Online]. Available: Http://ncte.org/standards/thelist.html [1999]. Extracts reprinted with permission: *Standards for the English Language Arts*, by the International Reading Association and the National Council of Teachers of English, Copyright 1996 by the International Reading Association and the National Council of Teachers of English.

National science education standards [Online]. Available: Http://books.nap.edu/html/nses [1999]. Extracts reprinted [adapted] with permission from *National Science Education Standards.* Copyright (1996) by the National Academy of Sciences. Courtesy of the National Academy Press, Washington, DC.

National standards for arts education [Online]. Available: Http://artsedge.kennedy-center.org/forms/arts1.html [1999]. Excerpts and adaptations used by permission from *National Standards for Arts Education.* Copyright 1994 by Music Educators National Conference.

Oakes, J. & Lipton, M. (1990). *Making the best of schools: A handbook for parents, teachers, and policymakers.* New Haven, CT: Yale University Press.

Ogden, E. H. & Germinario, V. (1995). *The nation's best schools: Blueprints for excellence.* Lancaster, PA.: Technomic Publishing Company, Inc.

Standards and position statements. (1997). National Council for the Social Studies (NCSS) [Online]. Available: Http://www.ncss.org/standards/home.html [1999].

Standards for foreign language learning [Online]. Available: Http://www.actfl.org/htdocs/standards/standards.htm [2000]. Extracts reprinted with permission from National Standards in Foreign Language Education Project (1999). *Standards for Foreign Language Learning in the 21st Century.* Yonkers, NY: National Standards in Foreign Language Education Project.

CHAPTER 4

Case Studies

This chapter will demonstrate the processes that we have recommended for evaluating the effectiveness of a high school for an individual student. We have included three case studies, one for each of the following types of high school: a small regional high school in a rural area, a large suburban high school, and an urban high school. For each case study we have described a different type of student and considered the effectiveness of the school for that particular student. The schools were selected using the process described in Chapter 2. We expected to find good schools and we did.

Schools vary from one to another in many ways and, although the general fundamental school characteristics need to be considered, so do those special characteristics of particular relevance to an individual student with particular needs and interests. Each case study, then, demonstrates the school assessment process using a prospective student as the focus. We have not done this to suggest that the school is limited to serving one type of student. In fact, we make an effort with each evaluation to indicate otherwise. For another type of student, the conclusion about the school's effectiveness may be different.

The questions and observations given in Chapter 3 are, of course, recommendations. The reality of an on-site visit is that time is limited. It is also intended for individual students, with the proper "fit" for those individuals being sought. So, it will be important to focus the questions/observations on what can best be learned from an on-site experience. We recommended in Chapter 2 that you request all available information prior to the visit so that you will arrive at the school informed. Thus, one's questions will vary depending upon the data provided ahead of time and depending on the individual student. The length of the visit has a big effect on what is learned on-site. Our shortest visit of two hours was for Case Study 2, where we were simulating a "typical parent visit" and were able to confidently determine that the school would be a good match for the prospective student. If you have done your homework well, then the visit will be productive, no matter what length. We did appreciate the longer visits because we were able to have a wider variety of experiences. There is a balance between listening to the school's presentation and asking appropriate questions. Having your questions written down ahead of time will also facilitate the visit.

Be sure to refer to Appendix C for a list of recommended materials that you should bring to the visit. If you decide to enroll your child in the school, these materials will facilitate the enrollment and course selection process tremendously.

Each case study follows the outline of effective education categories that appears in Appendix A. You may try to assess a category with a few selected questions. For example, with one school visit we assessed the category of parent/community relations by learning about parent/school team meetings that focus on the academic progress of the individual student. We were interested that the parent is involved at a very early stage when there is an academic concern. With this information available to us we did not pursue other aspects of parental involvement (e.g., PTA/PTO or parent volunteers). We had to keep in mind that our time was limited and other categories needed to be covered.

It is recommended that the school be visited during the academic year when the students are there to obtain an accurate view of the school. A typical school visit may last only about 45 minutes to an hour. Parents may wish to visit the school first and bring the student to a second visit. The student might request to spend time in a particular classroom or in a cocurricular activity. The individual school may have a recommended person to conduct the tour of the school. In Chapter 3 we recommended the principal as the requested person for this purpose. In fact, for two schools that we visited the guidance counselor was the contact person.

Brief visits to several classrooms and informal discussions with particular teachers may be recommended by the school rather than attempting to evaluate the teaching–learning situation based on one or two classroom observations. One brief snapshot of a classroom will not be a sufficient indication of the overall curriculum, nor will it provide a comprehensive view of the teaching–learning situation. Observations made from outside of the classroom without interrupting the session can reveal organization, interaction, and classroom management. Brief conversations with many members of the school provide an overall view of the school community—knowledge, curiosity, interest, enthusiasm, respect, concern for others. One can learn a lot from observing the interactions between school community members.

For each case study to follow, the effective education categories are divided into sections: what we learned from all of the data provided, what we wanted to learn during the visit, what we learned on-site, and a concluding summary within each category. The individual student is kept in mind throughout the evaluation. Again, different conclusions may be arrived at for different students. For example, the size of the school may be better for one type of student than for another. An overall conclusion, based on the prospective student, is given at the end of each case.

Assessment indicators are assigned where necessary. We felt that this would be helpful in reviewing each category for the overall evaluation of the school for the prospective student. The indicators are:

* = very good

+ = good

^ = possibly problematic

We cannot stress enough how valuable a visit to the school is. Although one can obtain good descriptive information about the school, the sense of "knowing" if a school is the right match for the child comes together during the visit. The opportunity to experience the climate of the school and to meet the school professionals and the students is an important one. During the school visits we were able to learn much that we could not have learned merely from the data provided. The feeling of the school (or the school climate) was an important ingredient in our assessment. Other examples include: observing the attentiveness and involvement of both teachers and students; observing the organization and orderliness of the school in process; the opportunity to meet and speak with many school personnel, including the superintendent, principal, counselors, office staff, security officials, curriculum supervisors/directors, teachers, and students; the opportunity to observe the facilities; the opportunity to see technology in use for various, integrated purposes; observing the recognition given to students and faculty throughout the school and for various reasons; and the opportunity to observe the strong use of the school library media center by the students. A visit to the school will tell you much.

Case Study 1
A Small Regional High School in a Rural Area:
Delaware Valley Regional High School
Frenchtown, New Jersey

Student Description. The prospective student for this high school was of average academic ability and needed special education assistance, particularly with math. The student had an interest in music and theater.

Before the Visit. Two websites were examined prior to the visit: the state-created school report card and the Delaware Valley Regional High School website. The website for the school's report card provided data for four years so we were able to compare data and note consistencies. A very helpful feature of the report card is the definition accompanying each section. We were also given the following information by the school: the Course Guide; the School Profile; a newsletter distributed to the community; the Student/Parent Handbook; Clubs, Activities, Sports; School Health Services and Athletic Physical Policies; and the Student Handbook.

The School Visit. Delaware Valley Regional High School serves students who have completed their K–8 schooling in one of five autonomous schools in the region. The actual area served by the high school is 88.9 square miles. The rural community is primarily residential and made up of a fairly homogeneous middle-income population of approximately 16,500. Each "feeding school" is dependent on the budget approval of its local township or borough. Hence, the opportunities within each feeding school vary, depending on local support. The regional high school is responsible for educating students who arrive at the school from varied educational experiences. However, there is a well-coordinated regional curriculum that all the feeding schools and the high school participate in. Delaware Valley Regional High School is located in a rural setting on a large piece of land. It is a one-story school, with the original building dating to 1959, and very well maintained. The school received a small addition in 1969 and in 1977 the library and a second gymnasium were added. The school design includes courtyards between classroom wings. There is an open feeling to the school due to both the exposure to the courtyards and the amount of natural light that is available in the school. The school design has an organized flow and it is very easy to "find one's way" within it. There are two main entrances to Delaware Valley Regional High School: one leads to the superintendent's office and the other to the main high school office. The school's mission statement is prominently displayed at one of the entrances.

We were met by a very friendly office staff and began our visit by checking in and receiving a visitor's pass.

The principal had recommended that the guidance counselor who works with the special education students be our contact person. The guidance counselor greeted us very warmly and was quick to introduce us to everyone we met throughout the visit. We spoke with the guidance counselor for about a half an hour and the remainder of our three-hour visit took place with a tour of the school. During the tour we met and spoke with teachers and students. We briefly visited many classrooms, the school library media center, the cafeteria and the auditorium.

ORGANIZATIONAL AND ADMINISTRATIVE VITALITY/EFFECTIVENESS

What we learned from all the data provided:

The school's mission statement is: "The mission of Delaware Valley Regional High School is to educate and guide students to achieve their fullest potential and become contributing members of society."

* Student Attendance rate is very good (94.9 percent, compared with the state's rate of 92.6 percent). The rate has steadily improved over the four-year period.

* Student/Administrator Ratio is low (140:1, compared with the state's average of 181:1). This is an asset because the administration has the opportunity to be more "in touch" with the student population.

* Number of Faculty/Administrator (10:1, compared with the state's average of 9.5:1). This is a reasonable ratio.

+ Administrators' Median Salary ($70,583, compared with the state's average of $82,375). This reflects both the years of service of the administration and the community's ability/willingness to support the administrators.

* Administrators' Years of Experience (twenty-three compared with the state's average of twenty-six).

* Code "C" Emergency Response Plan is being implemented.

* All doors are locked from the outside during the school day. Visitors must enter through the District and Main Office doors, sign in, and wear name tags in the school.

* Policies are clearly given in the Student/Parent Handbook. They include: Attendance Policy; information about the Health Curriculum/Family Life Education; Graduation Requirements; Marking System Explanation; Student Conduct Code Philosophy; Conduct Code Point System; Rights and Responsibilities of students, administrators, teachers, parents, and guardians.

* Examples of communication from both the superintendent and principal were given: the community newsletter and the Student/Parent Handbook. Both include forward-looking communications that demonstrate vision, high expectations, and the need for parental support.

What we wanted to learn during the visit:

Is time protected for teachers and students to stay on the task of learning?
How is a safe environment ensured?
What evidence is there that the mission of the school is communicated?
What is the general sense of organization in the school?

What we learned on-site:

* The school mission statement appears at the entrance to the school.
* The school facility is very well maintained, clean, and orderly. The building is relatively old, yet has been upgraded to a high level technologically.
* The school climate is very friendly, personable, and receptive. There is an open, approachable feeling in the school and the sense of community within is evident. The faculty and staff are very focused on the students. This was evident to us from the manner in which the students are spoken to—very candidly and respectfully.
* When asked if the school is a safe place, we were told that all schools are reassessing the safety of their schools following recent violence in schools across the country. The school does not face major problems in this area, but cannot afford to be complacent. Doors other than the two main entrances to the building are locked to outsiders and visitors must register in the main office and wear name tags.
* The hall atmosphere is well ordered. We observed students changing classes in a calm, unstressed, unusually quiet fashion. The students were prompt in arriving for classes and each class began smoothly and in a timely way.
* The principal is very involved in the workings of the school and very realistic about the goals of the school. He is appreciative and encouraging of the professional staff and, as an example, complimented the guidance staff on their high level of involvement. He explained the decision process that takes place prior to introducing AP course offerings and was realistic about the appropriate timing of such decisions.
* When asked if students might at times give tours of the school to prospective students, the principal expressed concern about the interference with their academic schedule. (Tours are given at one time during the year by students to the incoming freshman class.)

Concluding summary:

Delaware Valley Regional High School is extremely well organized and its leadership very competent and focused on learning. We learned this both from the written data that included communications from the administration and by what we observed in person.

The following reinforced our positive conclusion:

- Positive statistical data for this category
- Safe environment
- Protection of time for learning
- Well-ordered environment
- Knowledgeable, involved principal
- Extremely positive school climate

Naturally, these characteristics would be effective for any student and are excellent for the student described.

INSTRUCTIONAL ENVIRONMENT (TEACHERS AND LEARNERS)

What we learned from all the data provided:

* The size of the school is small (approximately 800 students).

* Average class size is small (nineteen, compared with the state's average of twenty-one). (This is defined by the school report card as the "average number of students assigned to a homeroom.") The number has fluctuated, but nearly always has been smaller than the state's average.

* The Student Mobility Rate is very low (2.7 percent, compared with the state's average of 3.8 percent). This indicates a stable environment in the school.

* Student/Faculty Ratio is low (11.5:1, compared with the state's average of 11.7:1). This is further evidence of a small class size.

+ Revenues for the district by percentage (It appears from the following data that local support could be improved.)

	Local Taxes	State	Federal	Other
District	62	35	1	2
State	64	29	1	6

^ Per Pupil Expenditures: $8,966 as compared with the state's average of $9,962. This is low compared with the state, but has increased significantly from the expenditure of four years earlier. (Faculty salaries and benefits are included in this expenditure. Faculty salaries can reflect the cost of living of the area.)

* Faculty Attendance Rate is high (97 percent, compared with the state's average of 96.9 percent).

* Faculty Academic Degrees: BA = 41%, MA = 58%, PhD = 1%.

+ Faculty Median Salary: $50,798 as compared with the state's average of $55,411. This is low in view of the following data that indicates that the faculty has been stable and the salaries should reflect those years of service.

* Faculty Years of Experience: twenty, compared with the state's average of seventeen. This reflects stability.

* The Art Teacher was honored by the governor for dedicated service.

* Professional development opportunities are provided by the county's "Educational Technology Training Center" to train classroom teachers for a technologically changing classroom. The center has partnerships with another school district and a university.

* The Course Guide and the school's website encourage student participation in the individual's curriculum design.

* The Course Guide describes the Supervised Study program that is designed to support classified students in their subject area classes.

What we wanted to learn during the visit:

Is the classroom atmosphere well ordered?

Is there clear organization to the teaching–learning process?

Do the teachers display an enjoyment of learning?

Is there an opportunity for different learning environments?

Are students learning how to seek information and locate additional resources?

Is there evidence of rigor and persistence?

What evidence is there of affective behaviors in the students: interest, intrinsic motivation, self-concept?

How is the individual developed in areas of responsibility and expressiveness?

What we learned on-site:

* We spoke with a student about the Family Life Education course and he talked with confidence about the practicality of the learning experience. This was one example of many interactions with students who were excited and curious about what they were learning.

* We briefly observed many classrooms and they were always orderly, with an engaged learning process. This was true whether the class was in discussion with teachers, pursuing independent projects, or in a study hall. The sense of alertness and focus to the task at hand was evidence that the students take their job of learning seriously.

* There is a very individualized approach to each student. The academic placement of each student is carefully considered and students may have quite a variety of academic levels in their course schedules. Students are encouraged to the higher academic levels wherever possible, but the decision is up to the student.

* If there is a need to make an academic course change for a student (e.g., to a different academic level), the change takes place when it is recognized and throughout the year. There is no delay until the next academic year. This process is more likely to be possible within a smaller school environment and certainly is an advantage of being in a smaller school.

* Responsibility is expected of the students. At the beginning of the freshman year an academic planning book is given to the students for noting assignments and encouraging responsibility for the completion of tasks. When we visited one of the classrooms we asked one student what the school was teaching them. He responded (unprompted!) that he was learning to be responsible for himself.

* Collaborative learning is strongly encouraged. An example of a collaborative learning experience is the combination of a special education teacher with a subject teacher. In this situation, a special education teacher will be present in the subject classroom to primarily offer support for classified special education students. The Special Education Coordinator organizes the collaborative learning experiences and, due to the success of the program, is asked by an increasing number of faculty to offer the experience in their classrooms.

* In the biology class we visited there was an obvious respectful, positive relationship between the students and the teacher. In fact, this student–teacher respect was consistent throughout the visit.

* In a music class students who had just performed a winter concert the evening before enthusiastically sang one of the pieces from the program for us.

* The class sizes that we observed were small as we had expected from the data provided.

* The visual arts curriculum is strong and student work is regularly displayed in a large area in the school library media center.

* Our interactions with each teacher were informative. Each teacher spoke with excitement about his or her subject area. Those teachers we were able to talk with at some length offered thorough descriptions of the curriculum as it would relate to the prospective student.

* We observed an active independent researching environment in the school library media center.

Concluding summary:

The instructional environment is most impressive and especially effective for the special education student described. This was evidenced by:

Small school size

Small class size

Stable environment (low student mobility)

Engaged, well-educated faculty

Well-ordered classrooms

Emphasis on student responsibility

Demonstrated researching skills by students

Serious, focused, curious, enthusiastic student population

Alertness to appropriate academic placement

Excellent support for special education students

Respectful, positive relationships between students and teachers

RICHNESS OF THE CURRICULUM

What we learned from all the data provided:

* The curriculum includes offerings for honors, college preparatory and general levels of study. A good number of course selections are available to meet the remedial needs of our prospective student, particularly in math where it is most needed.

* Language Arts: From our review of the course guide, several of the National Council of Teachers of English (NCTE) Standards are being met. A wide range of texts is being read that includes fiction, nonfiction, classic and contemporary works, as well as literature from many periods (the Greeks, the Bible, Shakespeare, British literature, American literature from John Smith to contemporary writers). The opportunity for writing in order to communicate with different audiences and for a variety of purposes exists (research paper, yearbook, imaginative writing, expository writing, journalism skills, poetry interpretations, critical evaluations, mass media writing). The research process is incorporated into the program. Students are learning to participate as "knowledgeable, reflective, creative, and critical members of a variety of literary communities" (NCTE Standards). They are reading literature, learning writing skills for several purposes, and learning to make connections between, in particular, reading and writing.

* Mathematics: All the National Council of Teachers of Mathematics (NCTM) Standards appear to be met with this broad curriculum offering. There is consistent reference to problem-solving skills and practical application of the mathematical knowledge. Curricular offerings are available for many career goals, including computer science.

* Social Studies: From the description of the course offerings, most of the National Council for the Social Studies (NCSS) Standards are reflected in the curriculum. In particular, there seems to be a focus on exposure to different cultures, an emphasis on research and reading of multiple sources, the opportunity to apply knowledge to modern-day problems, and an emphasis on the responsibilities of citizens. Electives provide the opportunity for two service learning projects and exposure to "contemporary patterns of human behavior" (NCSS Standards) within several courses.

* Science: There is an emphasis on inquiry (Content Standard A of the National Science Education Standards) in every course description regardless of the academic level. Also emphasized is the strong relationship between science

and mathematics. Personal health (part of Content Standard F) is well covered within the physical education component of the curriculum. Each of the other standards appears to be well covered, including confronting local, national, and global challenges to science and technology (part of Content Standard F). In a particularly creative course description (for Biological Science Curriculum Study) the history and nature of science (Content Standard G) is covered in depth. Students taking science courses at this high school will have multiple opportunities to be actively engaged in doing science.

* The Arts: All visual arts courses are electives and career possibilities are explored within each course. The visual arts courses, which appear from the course descriptions to be primarily product-oriented, do include the elements of art history, criticism, and aesthetics. Additional art courses are contained within the industrial technology curriculum, which offers media communications/printing, media communications/production, four woodworking courses, beginning drawing, technical drawing, engineering drawing, and architectural drawing. Theater courses (Performing Arts I & II) are offered within the English curriculum (the courses offer training in stage techniques, stage history, pantomime, characterization, scenes, and play production). Several music opportunities exist (band, music analysis and appreciation, chorus and advanced chorus). Thus there is ample opportunity for students to communicate "their thoughts and feelings in a variety of modes" (National Standards for Arts Education). The emphasis in the course offerings on the student's individual growth and creative expression is also in keeping with national standards.

* Information Literacy: Delaware Valley Regional High School's web page offers remote access to the library's resources that include: *Encyclopedia Britannica Online*, Proquest Direct, Electric Library, Infotrac, Contemporary Authors/Contemporary Literary Criticism/Discovering Authors, SIRS Researcher, Facts on File, and many carefully selected websites for both students and teachers. There is a full-time school library media center specialist.

* Foreign Language: Students in the "feeding schools" do offer a foreign language. The high school offers French (four years), German (four years), Latin (two years), and Spanish (four years).

* Transition to Work Programs: Career opportunities are a part of much of the curriculum. In addition to courses mentioned earlier are course offerings in accounting and business mathematics and several industrial technology courses (including media communications/printing, four woodworking courses, technical drawing and two architectural drawing courses).

+ Moral Education: Although this does not appear to be specifically built into the curriculum, the school's standards are clearly stated in the Student/Parent Handbook and both conflict resolution and preventative programs are in effect.

What we wanted to learn during the visit:

Math curriculum: How effective is the program for special education students?

Science curriculum: How is the curriculum developed? Are field trips provided to promote an opportunity for on-site scientific inquiry?

How is technology integrated into the curriculum?

What are the expectations for study beyond the classroom?

Is there an equitable opportunity for each student in the school; that is, how does the school serve the varying educational needs of the student population?

How is the school library media center integrated into the curriculum?

What we learned on-site:

* The coordinator of the Mathematics and Computer Science curriculum described the success of the collaborative teaching partnership. She herself has a background of working with special education students and encourages the partnership created in the classroom with the combination of subject faculty and special education faculty. The benefits for the special education students are documented.

* Collaborative learning experiences, which promote conceptual learning, are offered by combining courses from different subject areas of the curriculum.

* AP courses are continuing to be added. The Spanish AP course was added once there was a sufficient number of students eligible for the AP course.

+ There are opportunities for further vocational training at another location rather than exclusively on-site. Academic classes are held at the Delaware Valley Regional High School and a bus then transports the students in the afternoon to another facility that is shared by more than one high school for the vocational training.

* Curriculum revision by the teachers is frequent. We were informed of a recent revision that proposed a marine science course.

* In a woodworking class we observed the use of technology integrated into the curriculum. Students first design their projects using a computer program and then execute the design in wood.

* The school library media center integrates research instruction with course assignments. The library is open to students and faculty during all of the school hours and the library is an active learning environment. Electronic access to research materials (periodical databases, the library's book collection, and web resources) is very good (as described in the section, "Richness of the Curriculum").

* There is a television studio housed in the school library media center.

* There are several types of study halls. Some are especially designed for special education students. The teacher assigned to the study hall works with the students on homework assignments. Sometimes homework is begun within class time so that the students have an opportunity to ask for help at the beginning stages of their homework.

+ As with many schools, the number of field trips is lower than in the past due to the cost of such trips so, for example, field trips for science exploration are not done as frequently. Field trips have been included in the proposal for the Marine Science course.

Concluding summary:

A smaller school will naturally have a smaller curricular offering due to both the number of students and the number of faculty. The range of course offerings at this relatively small school is quite extensive and offers much to all levels of academic ability. For the student described the variety of offerings is more than adequate and the opportunity to participate simultaneously in courses at different academic levels is a definite plus. The math curriculum offers several courses to the "general" level student that appear to be particularly rich offerings for the average math student. The student's music interest can be well met by band, music analysis and appreciation, chorus and advanced chorus. And the student's theater interest can be met both by the Performing Arts I & II courses and by the cocurricular activities discussed ahead in "Student Life" (Thespians and Drama Productions).

ACADEMIC ACHIEVEMENT

What we learned from all the data provided:

* High School Proficiency Test/Grade 11: The results are considerably higher than the state's average (87.3, compared with the state's average of 75.3). However, the results in each area (reading, mathematics, and writing) have declined slightly over a four-year period.

* Scholastic Aptitude Test Results: Math (average score) = 542 (There has been steady improvement in this score over a four-year period.). Verbal (average score) = 532 (This score has been fairly consistent over a four-year period).

* Number of Students taking the SAT has increased to 80 percent over a four-year period reflecting a greater interest in a college education.

* Advanced Placement Tests were given in biology, chemistry, English literature and composition, government and politics–U.S., Mathematics–Calculus AB, physics B, U.S. history. The following AP courses have been recently introduced: Psychology (9/99), Computer Science (9/00), Spanish (9/00). Significantly, ten students were named as AP Scholars by the College Board.

* Honors Programs: Gifted and Talented (four courses), Honors English I, II, III, Honors Algebra I & II, Chemistry Science/Engineering, Honors BCCS Biology, Honors Geometry, PSSC Physics, Honors Analysis, U.S. History I–Honors, World History–Honors.

* There is an Academic Hall of Fame (for students who earn a 90 average or better for all 16 marking periods of high school).

+ Post-Graduation Plans:

Four–year college/university = 56%

Two–year college = 28%

Other postsecondary school = 6%

Military = not reported

Full-time employment = 7%

Other = 3%

What we wanted to learn during the visit:

How is student progress communicated to parents?

What we learned on-site:

* The Academic Hall of Fame is emphasized in two locations in the school: at the entrance to the school and in the school library media center. A photograph of each student in the Academic Hall of Fame is displayed.

* Parents are quite involved in the academic monitoring of the students. There are regular communications from teachers to parents about the progress of students and many use e-mail and voice mail for this purpose. The communications are informative and frequent. The communications are both supportive and in recognition of academic difficulties. Again, a smaller school allows this opportunity for frequent, informal communication between teachers and parents.

* We attended a traditional holiday tea that was organized by the honor students, demonstrating further recognition of this academically successful group of students.

Concluding summary:

The academic progress is very favorable, with a steadily increasing student interest in a college education. This is supported visibly in the school by the Academic Hall of Fame in two locations. Parents are strongly involved in the support of the academic program and communications about academic progress are effectively made. For the prospective student there is a strong academic opportunity and encouragement for high academic achievement.

SUPPORT FOR LEARNING

What we learned from all the data provided:

* A Student Handbook is given to each freshman and is intended for individual planning. It also provides useful resources including studying strategies and an extensive guide to writing a research paper.

* Students and parents are well informed about the need to meet with the guidance counselor for several purposes: vocational and career information, college and scholarship counseling, personal problems, testing, written recommendations, and references. Students and parents are encouraged to communicate frequently with the guidance counselors.

+ Expenditures for the classroom—general supplies/textbooks, purchased services, and other: $343 per pupil, compared with the state's average of $296 per pupil. (This amount is currently significantly better than the state's average, but represents a dramatically positive trend over earlier years. Prior to this the amounts were significantly lower than the state's average.)

What we wanted to learn during the visit:

What technological opportunities exist in the school?
How do the guidance counselors support the teaching and learning process?

What we learned on-site:

* The guidance counselor who gave us a tour of the school impressed us very favorably. It was obvious that he is very "in touch" with the students and parents and is alert to the academic progress of the students. While passing one student in the hallway he inquired about a recent college visit and asked the student to make an appointment with him soon to discuss his college search. The guidance counselors play a crucial role in the academic decision-making process of students and it is very obvious that the guidance counselors here are very proactive.

* There are proactive and responsive counseling activities. In response to a recent automobile accident in which a student was killed one of the counselors conducted several group sessions with students, including sessions at the accident site. The student who died had been DUI and this fact encouraged a student to form a chapter of SADD at the high school.

* There are several computer drops in every classroom. We observed the use of computers in the foreign language lab, woodworking classes, industrial arts class, business classes, and in the school library media center.

+ We asked about resource support for instruction (classroom—general supplies/textbooks, purchased services) because the support was historically weak, even though it has recently improved significantly. In general, instructional equipment is adequate, though modest in some areas.

Concluding summary:

We were especially impressed with the strong proactive guidance support. Further support for learning, the Supervised Study Program, is discussed in the category "Richness of the Curriculum." The availability of technology and (most important) the academic role that technology is taking in this school is very impressive. The school library media center is an active learning environment with excellent resources that are being used. Although there could be additional resource support, the existing support is very good and more than meets the needs of the prospective student.

STUDENT LIFE

What we learned from all the data provided:

* Dropout rate is very low (1.6 percent, compared with the state's average of 3.8 percent).
* The following clubs and activities are offered: Academic Achievement Society, Art Club, Band, Calculus League, Choir, Delphi, Drama Productions, Environmental Club, International Club, Key Club, Mock Trial, National Honor Society, Peer Leadership, Poetry Club, SAT Prep, Ski Club, Stage Crew, Student Council, Thespians, School Yearbook, Varsity Club, Academic Meet, and Winter Guard (a branch of the marching band).
+ The following sports are offered: *Fall*: cross-country (both boys and girls), cheerleading, field hockey, football, soccer (both boys and girls). *Winter*: cheerleading, basketball (both boys and girls), wrestling. *Spring*: baseball, track (both boys and girls), girls' softball, golf.

What we wanted to learn during the visit:

How active are students in cocurricular activities?

What we learned on-site:

* The members of the Thespian Society are listed on a plaque at the entrance of the school.
* There is an active theater program (Drama Productions) that is open to all students. Three plays are performed each academic year.
* Student involvement is active and evident throughout Delaware Valley Regional High School. For example, students contribute daily to the school's web page, students are very involved in cocurricular activities, and in general there was an enthusiasm from the students that came across throughout the day for both academic and cocurricular activities.

Concluding summary:

The very low dropout rate is a positive indicator that the students feel they have a stake in their school. The positive school climate mentioned earlier also supports this. There is a good number and variety of cocurricular activities that have attracted a good number of students. Our prospective student's interest in music would be met both through the academic music program (observed in the category "Richness of the Curriculum") and by the opportunity to participate in the band or choir. In addition to the academic offerings (Performing Arts I & II), the student's interest in theater would be met by participation in either drama productions or stage crew and the student could earn an induction into Thespians. We want to mention here the advantage of a smaller school for cocurricular opportunities. Although the number of offerings may be smaller than a larger school could provide, the opportunity to be involved will be greater due to the smaller number of students who "compete" for a place in the activity.

PARENT/COMMUNITY RELATIONS

What we learned from all the data provided:

* Delaware Valley Regional High School's website is an excellent communication tool to the community. New information about the happenings of the school appears daily.

* The Course Guide very clearly emphasizes the important role of parental input into their child's academic considerations.

* The Student/Parent Handbook communicates clearly the expectations of the school.

What we wanted to learn during the visit:

How are parents involved in the school?

What we learned on site:

* As discussed earlier in the categories "Academic Achievement" and "Support for Learning," there is frequent communication with parents from both teachers and guidance counselors.

Concluding summary:

The introduction of the World Wide Web, voice mail, and e-mail provides a greater opportunity for communication with parents and to the community about the school's effectiveness. In addition, the community receives a newsletter highlighting special features of Delaware Valley Regional High School. It is clear to us that parents, in particular, are strongly encouraged to be a part of the academic program. This serves our prospective student well since parental support for special education needs can be especially needed.

OVERALL SUMMARY FOR CASE STUDY 1

The prospective student would be served very well by Delaware Valley Regional High School. It is clear that support for special education is taken quite seriously and there are multiple opportunities for the student to be supported: the Supervised Study Program (which includes collaborative learning and special education study halls), the support by the special education guidance counselor, and the encouragement by the school for parental support. The small school is a plus to ensure that this particular student does not "get lost." The calm and friendly school climate is an asset to learning for this student as well. And the small school environment also allows for greater opportunities for inclusion in cocurricular activities, particularly music and theater. The school obviously serves many types of students well and is significantly growing in the area of academic achievement and encouragement for higher education. Students respond well to high goals set for them and Delaware Valley Regional High School lives up to the goals set in its mission statement "to educate and guide students to achieve their fullest potential and become contributing members of society."

Case Study 2
A Large Suburban High School:
Council Rock High School
Newtown, Pennsylvania

Student Description. The student we considered for this school has an excellent academic achievement record with particular interests in social studies, mathematics, and English. The student wants to pursue opportunities for Honors and AP courses. The student is also curious about cocurricular activities related to the areas listed.

Before the Visit. One website was examined: the state-created school profile. Materials that were given to us for review were: School Profile (created by Council Rock High School), Program Planning Guide, Graduation Project description, Co-curricular Directory, and a brochure on Conflict Resolution as it is practiced in the high school. The website School Profile provided information for one academic year. Definitions of the "School Profile Indicators" were given.

The School Visit. Council Rock High School is located on the edge of a suburban town in an ethnically homogeneous school district located 25 miles from a major northeastern city. The approximate school district population of 60,000 within 72 square miles consists of middle- to upper middle-income families with a wide variety of occupational and educational backgrounds. The school building is a two-story structure designed in a two-winged parallel fashion, and is fairly new. Each wing is nearly identical in its layout. The building supports sophisticated facilities, including an indoor swimming pool. We entered through the designated entrance and were met by a very friendly staff member who asked that we sign in as visitors and gave us a visitor tag to wear throughout the school.

The principal had recommended that a guidance counselor be our contact person for the visit. The guidance counselor was very enthusiastic and well prepared for our visit with many suggestions for parents. Many of these suggestions appear in Appendix C. The checklist that she recommends will save parents much time when transferring to a new school. We learned that there are quite a few families who move into the area due to corporate moves and the experience of introducing new students to the high school is not a new one. The counselor remembers a not-so-distant past when many of the students were the children of farmers and had quite a bit of work to do each morning before they arrived at school. This type of student is very unusual today.

We were at Council Rock High School for about two hours and spent most of that time talking with the counselor, who had much to share with us. The tour that we took of the school took place toward the end of the school day. We were able to observe classroom activities from outside the classroom and observed a variety of such situations: a history class, music class, computer labs where instruction was taking place, physical education classes, art class, and the school library media center.

ORGANIZATIONAL AND ADMINISTRATIVE VITALITY/EFFECTIVENESS

What we learned from all the data provided:

* Student attendance rate is very good in the district (the school's rate is not given, but the district rate is 96.3 percent, compared with the state's rate of 93.9 percent).

There are five assistant principals. We noted in the cocurricular directory that two of the assistant principals are responsible for the Athletic Directorship and the Student Activities Program.

* The Suburban One League Code of Conduct appears at the beginning of the Co-Curricular Directory.

* Conflict resolution is supported by the school by a peer mediation program.

What we wanted to learn during the visit:

What is the role of each of the assistant principals?
What are the key expectations communicated by the principal?
How does the school ensure a safe and orderly environment?

What we learned on-site:

* The principal shared his philosophy of the school with us. He believes in a smaller high school environment than this one and works very hard to create and maintain the feeling of a smaller school here. He supports the upcoming building of a second high school in the district that will drastically reduce the size of the current school (current enrollment for grades 10 to 12 is 2,636). He is equally concerned with both the academic development and the development of the students as citizens and leads the faculty in upholding this philosophy. The administration is very visible within Council Rock High School. Almost unbelievably (because the school is so large), the principal and the assistant principals are very "hands on," eating lunch daily with the students and meeting with students at their request. He mentioned that the school library media center had recently been relocated just outside his office and that he was very pleased to have a window in his office that looked out on the new facility.

It was clear that he is very much in touch with the student population and encourages the faculty to do the same.

* We were greeted in a very friendly manner by all the personnel we encountered at the school. Although the enrollment is very high, there is a strong community feeling and one does not have the sense of being in an overwhelmingly large environment. The climate is quite stimulating.

The assistant principals are responsible for each of the grade levels and for budgeting, scheduling, attendance, athletic programs, student activities, peer mediation, and discipline.

* When asked about the safety within the school we were told that the administration is very proactive and does not tolerate misbehavior. Each Grade Level Assistant Principal is responsible for peer mediation and discipline. Parents are notified in the event of any incident.

Concluding summary:

From our conversation with the principal and our observations of the school we were impressed with the dynamic quality of the school leadership. With consistent leadership from the principal and assistant principals the members of the school community are very student focused. The extra effort made by the principal and the assistant principals to eat daily with students and work toward a "small school" feeling especially impressed us. The high attendance rate is evidence that the school is meeting the students' expectations. The prospective student would definitely benefit from this leadership style that promotes attention to the whole student, teaching citizenship as well as academics.

INSTRUCTIONAL ENVIRONMENT (TEACHERS AND LEARNERS)

What we learned from all the data provided:

The size of the three-year high school is large (2,636 students).

* The majority of the classes (78.3 percent) have twenty to thirty students enrolled.

* Enrollment is stable (96 percent of the students began attending the school before this school year).

* Student teacher ratio is approximately 1:20.

* Teacher absenteeism is low (2.9 percent for the school and 3.5 percent for the district).

Professional development pursued by teachers is listed as 1.1 percent of their contractual days.

What we wanted to learn during the visit:

We did not understand the description of professional development given at the School Profile website. It appeared to be quite low and we needed clarification.
What opportunities exist for different student learning environments?

What we learned on-site:

* We observed several different learning environments, from the traditional lecture/discussion style to students working independently and in small group settings. There was an obvious sense of purpose within each of these settings.
* Class size was in the twenties (as expected from the statistical data) and students were engaged within the classroom settings.
* The school library media center was very active, with a large number of students researching actively. Students were supporting each other in their research process and obviously quite capable of seeking information independently.
* School district professional development opportunities for teachers are frequent and ongoing throughout the academic year and continuing during the summer. Over 100 free professional development courses are offered to teachers during the summer.
* There were multiple exhibit cases in the school that celebrate the many achievements (both academic and cocurricular) of the students.

Concluding summary:

The learning environment appears to be very grounded. We based this conclusion on: small class sizes even though the enrollment is high, a stable environment, and low teacher absenteeism. A good number of continual professional development opportunities provide the teachers with constant professional stimulation throughout the year. Professional development strengthens the teaching–learning experience. Because our prospective student is academically outstanding, there will be a demand for knowledgeable, effective, intellectually curious teachers who believe in continual learning. There is an overall climate of purpose within Council Rock High School. We observed this in several settings when the students were exhibiting a sense of responsibility for their work at hand. It was clear that the students had been given a clear sense of direction by the teachers and were thus capable of independent work. Again, this learning environment would suit our prospective student well.

RICHNESS OF THE CURRICULUM

What we learned from all the data provided:

There are course offerings for multiple academic levels including remedial, low-to-average, average, college-bound, accelerated, and honors. For several course descriptions the estimated homework time is clearly stated. This awareness is an advantage when preparing a heavy academic schedule.

* Language Arts: The primary emphases in the required English courses (spanning the multiple academic levels previously noted) are on the following reading skills: word attack, factual and implied comprehension, and critical reading skills. Texts include novels, plays, poems, short stories, essays, literature from American genres, Shakespearean dramas, literary criticism, and literature of European writers. Films are introduced in at least one course offering. The following writing skills are taught: organization, proofreading, revising, sentence structure, paragraph development, and mechanics. Types of writing assignments include: expository writing related to the literature studied, short papers, literary research essay, critical essays analyzing literary selections, personal essays, creative papers, imaginative/descriptive writing, and practical writing. Speaking and listening are also a part of the Language Arts curriculum. Included in nearly every course description are emphases on grammar and usage, vocabulary, spelling, and for college-bound students (in grades 11 and 12) there is practice for the PSAT and SAT. For the average through honors level courses the research process plays a significant role, including the requirement of a research paper with documentation (from grade 11 on). At least one literature course is required by juniors and seniors who have not taken one of the required full-year English courses. The course selections include: American Literature, Ancient Mythology (Greek, Roman and Norse), Modern Poetry (1880–present), Mystery/Detective Literature (of the past 150 years), Science Fiction and Fantasy, Shakespeare's plays, World Literature, World Mythology (Middle Eastern, Far Eastern, Native American Indian, South American, and African cultures, legends of King Arthur and the Age of Chivalry). Other electives include "Individualized Communication" and "Public Speaking," offering the opportunity to further develop speaking communication skills. Examples of the requirements for these courses include: story mappings; the writing of an original myth or legend; researching an author's style, impact and thematic message, and delivering the findings in both a report and an oral presentation accompanied by one or more visual aids.

The following aspects of these courses correspond with the NCTE standards, most of which are met by these course offerings: The opportunity exists for students to read a wide range of print texts from many periods of both American and world literatures, primarily fiction. Assignments require students to interpret and evaluate their reading. It is clear that the courses emphasize writing for effective communication, primarily in response to literature read. The emphasis on research includes multiple available resources (as described later under "Information Literacy").

* Mathematics: The course descriptions are quite detailed, including a lengthy list of the topics to be covered in the course. Again, multiple academic levels are met by the offerings, which include courses from other departments as options for the mathematics graduation requirement. Three computer pro-

gramming courses are also offered to satisfy the graduation requirement (BA-SIC and C++ languages are taught). The emphasis in the NCTM standards on using mathematical knowledge is clearly discussed in the algebra and geometry course descriptions and in the following course descriptions: Applied Mathematics, Mathematics for Business, Financial Recordkeeping, Personal Finance, and Accounting. Specific references to demonstrated knowledge through reasoning and problem-solving skills are found in the algebra and geometry course descriptions. For the advanced mathematics student there are many options: Honors Geometry, Honors Analysis, and Analytic Geometry and Calculus (AP). Many mathematics courses require that the student have a graphing calculator.

* Social Studies: Most of the NCSS standards appear to be met in the course descriptions, particularly those at the college-bound level. Of interest to us was a required "Multicultural Studies" course. This course and the "Honors World Cultures" course reinforce the following thematic strands of the NCSS standards: "Culture"; "Time, Continuity and Change"; "People, Places and Environments"; and "Global Connections." Several psychology and sociology courses provide the opportunity to learn about the thematic strands of "Individual Development and Identity." The governing process appears to be most thoroughly taught in the Honors United States Government and Politics course. The thematic strand of "Production, Distribution and Consumption" should be met in the Honors Economic Theory course. Service learning is optional at Council Rock High School and is encouraged. The Gifted Program in the school's curriculum includes three courses in the Social Studies curriculum (Honors American Studies, Honors Survey of Western Thought, Honors Philosophy). Course descriptions refer to both primary and secondary sources, research through electronic media, and required reading in nontextbook sources, and "on-site" experiences.

* Science: Laboratory investigation is noted in most of the course descriptions, emphasizing the inquiry-based learning element of the courses. The dissection opportunities are quite sophisticated (fetal pig, sheep organs, cat). Most of the NSE standards appear to be met, although Space Science is not an evident part of the curriculum. Because the course descriptions emphasize laboratory investigations it is not clear whether the "History and Nature of Science" aspect of the NSE standards is as significant a part of the science curriculum. Small-group activity is emphasized in the Plant-Animal Growth and Development course. The "Science and Technology" standard is met by the courses: Fundamentals of Electricity and Electronics and Fundamentals of Power Technology. Unique course offerings include: Nuclear Science, three nutrition courses, and Behavioral Science-Experimental Psychology. Personal Health is taught within the Health curriculum, a requirement for students in the eleventh grade.

* The Arts: Visual Arts: The excellent course description for the introductory Art Department course, Essentials of Art, describes the focus on "princi-

ples of design which are foundations for visual art experiences." Knowledge of "relating art to everyday living in both a practical and aesthetic sense" is a course objective. The students will "experiment with problems relating to design elements" and find "personal solutions to art-based problems." All art courses offered feature four major areas of art: production, history, criticism, and aesthetics. Available courses for pursuing art education include sculpture, ceramics, jewelry, design, drawing, and painting. All are available at the basic, introductory, and advanced levels and a Drawing and Painting course is available at the Honors/Studio level. The music curriculum offers courses for the following performing groups: Band, Choir, and Orchestra. Two music theory courses concentrate on the building blocks of music (e.g., notation, study of the piano keyboard, major and minor scales, basic chord progressions of tonal music). Additional courses include: Honors Music Arranging, Guitar (three academic levels), and Improvisation. Theater courses are taught within the English curriculum and include Acting and Directing. Communications courses include: Broadcast Communications, TV Production, Filmmaking, Public Speaking and Broadcast Journalism. These courses, in particular the Essentials of Art course, offer the opportunity for the student to develop the following aspects of the National Standards for Arts Education: "learning artistic modes of problem solving," "understanding the influences of the arts," and "making decisions in situations where there are no answers." And students, with each of the many course offerings available, have the opportunity for "communicating their thoughts and feelings in a variety of modes" (*National Standards for Arts Education*).

   * Information Literacy: Clearly from the course descriptions, research and the utilization of the school library media center for that purpose are highly integrated into the curriculum. In addition, a graduation project is required to "assure that students are able to apply, analyze, synthesize, and evaluate information and communicate significant knowledge and understanding" (Council Rock High School Program Planning Guide). Library hours are offered beyond the hours of the school day to allow additional access. The goal of the library staff is to "develop students' skill in defining and solving problems, competence in finding and using information from a variety of sources, and enthusiastic attitudes toward libraries and reading for a lifetime" (Council Rock High School Program Planning Guide). There are two librarians in the school. Library resources include an estimated 25,200 titles (books, periodicals, pamphlets, maps, videotapes, films, software, and other electronic media). In addition, the library was selected by the State School Librarians Association for the 1993 Outstanding State School Library Media Program Award. The elements in the position statement of the AASL are nearly identical to the goals and requirements of Council Rock High School.

   * Foreign Language: Courses are offered for the following languages for levels 1 and 2: Latin; for levels 1, 2, and Honors 3 and 4: French, German, and Spanish.

* Transition to Work Programs: A half-day vocational program is available at a separate facility that is jointly operated by four participating school districts. The majority of the academic and cocurricular programs are offered by the high school. The vocational offerings at the vocational facility are structured in three divisions: Career Academy Division, Technical Division, and Academic Division. Courses in the Career Academy Division (designed exclusively for the college-bound student): Computer Sciences, Engineering and Related Technologies (in partnership with a major university) and Health Sciences (in partnership with a major university). Courses in the Technical Division: two automotive courses; Commercial Art and Design; two computer courses; Construction Carpentry; Cosmetology; Culinary Arts; Drafting and Design Technology; Early Childhood Care and Education; Electrical and Network Cabling Technology; Electronics Technology; Health Occupations; Heating, Ventilation, Air Conditioning and Refrigeration; Marketing and Management; Media and Communications Technology; Plumbing; Precision Machining Technology; Telecommunications Technology; Welding Technology. Courses in the Academic Division (one may be scheduled): Algebra I and II, Geometry, Advanced Mathematical Concepts. In addition, there is a cooperative work experience offered.

+ Moral Education: Voluntary service learning opportunities exist through several channels either under a formalized program or through student service organizations, student government, school projects, and individual student initiatives. This provides an opportunity for the student to "integrate individual interests and social responsibilities" (ASCD Panel on Moral Education). The conflict resolution program trains students to be peer mediators, thus weaving the program into the school's fabric. This also is in keeping with the ASCD recommendations. A code of conduct appears prominently at the beginning of the Co-curricular Directory, clearly outlining responsibilities for spectators at cocurricular activities. These expectations encourage a respectful climate.

What we wanted to learn during the visit:

We were curious to learn more details about the Graduation Project.

Realizing that the required graphing calculators are expensive, would they be provided by the school if a student could not afford one? What other tools are used for teaching math?

Have there been any recent curricular developments (e.g., new courses developed)?

What we learned on-site:

* As described in the previous section, "Organizational and Administrative Vitality/Effectiveness," the principal's educational philosophy is toward educating the "whole person." The principal and faculty model the behavior ex-

pected of the students and make themselves available to the students for both academic and support purposes. This speaks to a concern that moral education is an essential part of the school day, even if not specifically designated within the curriculum.

* In addition to the curriculum requirements the counselor we spoke with recommends that all students take the courses Strategies of Writing and Fundamentals of Information Technology.

* Course selection is done by students, but involves teacher, counselor, and parental input.

* Every new student is tested in math for the appropriate placement. Where appropriate, students are also tested for World Languages and Honors English. Testing is a key ingredient for accurate academic placement of students as a minimum of course changes can take place during the school year.

* There is a district curriculum and a district coordinator responsible for the coordination of each K–12 subject. Both teachers and students have input into curricular decisions. National, state, and school standards are involved in these decisions. A science fiction course was recently added to the curriculum based on input from students, teachers, and counselors.

* The Graduation Project is state-mandated but each school creates its own program within the state requirement. In Council Rock High School the project may be done within specifically designated courses. It is designed to assess initiative, questioning, problem-finding, problem-solving, the ability for independent research, the creation of a product or performance, mastery, and self-reflection. The research component not only encourages the inquiry process but the information-seeking process that is a lifelong learning skill.

* The offering of a Gifted Program is a state requirement. The choice for the Gifted Program to be centered in the Social Studies was based on student and faculty recommendation.

* Enrollment in Advanced Placement (AP) courses is based both on student interest and the recommendation of both the teacher and counselor.

* For students in advanced math courses there is a distance learning course available after calculus via Stanford University. The math teachers must have input into the decision for a student to be a part of this program. There are also partnership agreements with local colleges.

* Although students are expected to purchase their own graphing calculators, the school provides for those who do not have their own.

* Computers also serve as tools for the teaching of math.

* Students are encouraged to take World Languages for at least three, and, if possible, four years.

* Physical Education is required. Students select a different activity based on their interests each marking period. Health may be substituted for one of the activities.

* For students who are experiencing academic difficulty there are clinics after school every Tuesday and Thursday. The later buses will transport the students

home. Teachers are available at other times. Peer tutoring is done by National Honor Society students every Tuesday night in the library. There is also a list of private tutors made available to students. Study groups are also available.

Concluding summary:

A larger school can offer more in its curriculum; for the special interests of our prospective student (English, Mathematics, and Social Studies) there is not only a wide range of electives but Honors and AP courses. Of unique opportunity are the Gifted Program centered in the Social Studies curriculum and the advanced distance learning math course available via Stanford University. The evidence of student input into curricular development could prove to be an additional opportunity for our prospective student.

ACADEMIC ACHIEVEMENT

What we learned from all the data provided:

* Intended pursuits for graduates (1996–97): 90.9 percent intend to pursue postsecondary study at a degree-granting institution as compared with the state's percentage of 68.1 percent; (1997–98): 94.9 percent.
* CEEB Advanced Placement Participation:

Percent of 11th and 12th graders taking CEEB AP Exam:
English: 5.9 percent (compared with the state average of 3.0 percent)
Math/Computer Science: 5.2 percent (compared with the state average of 2.2 percent)
Science: 4.6 percent (compared with the state average of 2.1 percent)
Social Science/History: 5.7 percent (compared with the state average of 3.5 percent)
Art & Music: 0.1 percent (compared with the state average of 0.2 percent)
Languages: 2.9 percent (compared with the state average of 0.3 percent)
Percent of 11th and 12th graders scoring 3 or above on the exam:
English: 92.2 percent (compared with the state average of 71.0 percent)
Math/Computer Science: 90.1 percent (compared with the state average of 68.0 percent)
Science: 97.5 percent (compared with the state average of 61.4 percent)
Social Science/History: 77.8 percent (compared with the state average of 61.6 percent)
Art & Music: (not given) (compared with the state average of 72.0 percent)
Languages: 80.0 percent (compared with the state average of 64.4 percent)

* State System of School Assessment results for grade 11:

Mathematics Scores: 1510 (compared with the state average of 1300; and compared with similar schools' average of 1390–1460)
Reading Scores: 1430 (compared with the state average of 1300; and compared with similar schools' average of 1350–1400)

* Standardized Test results:

PSAT: Verbal: 51.2 and Math: 51.6
SAT: Verbal: 543 and Math: 564

* National Merit Scholarships:

	1997	1998	1999
Finalists	12	9	13
Semifinalists	13	11	14
Commended	20	34	23

* Students have been consistently recognized for academic achievement in state and national math competitions.
* Students have been consistently recognized for academic achievement in state and national writing competitions.
* Consistent superior ratings for the entire music program in local, state, national, and international festivals.

What we wanted to learn during the visit:

Are graduation requirements set by the state or are additional ones set for the high school?

What we learned on-site:

* Council Rock High School conforms to all state requirements for graduation, but has developed its own set of descriptions of requirements.
* Student class rank is computed by a point system. Courses are assigned points according to academic difficulty and complexity.
* Some of the colleges that students are attending after Council Rock High School include Pennsylvania State University, University of Pittsburgh, Bloomsburg University, University of Delaware, University of Maryland, and Westchester University. Students also attend Stanford University, Duke University, Boston University, and the University of Michigan.

Concluding summary:

There is no doubt that Council Rock High School is superb academically. Because our prospective student is college-bound, the academically oriented environment will provide an excellent preparation for college.

SUPPORT FOR LEARNING

What we learned from all the data provided:

* Technology Resources:

380 computers are available for student use (Computer-Student ratio = 1:7).

Computer labs and the Library/Media Center have access to the internet, Broadcast TV, and Cable TV.

^ Counselor-student ratio is high: 1:377.

What we wanted to learn during the visit:

Is there pressure on the counselor staff to provide adequate counseling to the students due to the high counselor-student ratio?

What we learned on-site:

+ Despite the relatively high counselor-student ratio there are many programs and services made available. Counselors assist students with college applications and write individualized recommendations for each student. There is an excellent recordkeeping system.

* There is a student partner system for new students, who are taken to classes and educated about the details of the school organization by their student partner.

* Students with financial needs will be loaned equipment (such as graphing calculators).

* Sophisticated resources are visible throughout the school (computer labs, school library media center, art materials, science resources, and athletic facilities).

Concluding summary:

The resources described here, in the introduction and in the section "Richness of the Curriculum," are more than adequate for our prospective student. Even though the counselor-student ratio is high, our interview with the guidance counselor gave us the confidence that academic planning is very thoroughly attended to and is a strong focus of the counselors' responsibilities. Academic planning is, of course, important for every student and our prospective student would be served well by this guidance team.

STUDENT LIFE

What we learned from all the data provided:

* Dropout rate is very low: 1.8 percent (compared with the state average of 4.2 percent)

* The following cocurricular activities are regularly offered:

Student Activities: AIDS Awareness, Art Forum, Artistic Design Club, Band Front (part of the marching band), Choral Groups, Class Activities (for each class in grades 10 through 12), Debate Club, Environmental Action Club, World Language Clubs, Future Business Leaders of America Club, School Newspaper, Instrumental Groups, Concert Jazz Band, Dixie Band, Marching/Concert Band, Orchestra, Symphonic Band, International Club, Intramurals, Key Club, Literary Club, Mathletes, National Honor Society, Political Science Club, Presidential Classroom Program, Drama Club (at least three major productions and from two to five smaller scale efforts), Stage Technicians, Student Executive Board (student governing body), Students Against Destructive Decisions (S.A.D.D.), Technology Club, Yearbook.

Athletic Program: *Fall: Both male and female*: cross-country, golf, *Male*: football, soccer, *Female*: cheerleading, field hockey, tennis, volleyball. *Winter*: *Both male and female*: basketball, bowling, swimming, track, *Male*: wrestling, *Female*: cheerleading, *Spring: Both male and female*: track and field, *Male*: baseball, tennis, volleyball, *Female*: lacrosse, soccer, softball.

* Superior award given to Concert Choir, Imperial Chapel Vienna-Austria Millennium, 1996.

* Superior award given to Marching Band at London Parade Festival, London, England, 1998.

* Recognized by the PIAA as one of the outstanding athletic programs in the state.

What we wanted to learn during the visit:

For the prospective student we wanted to know more about the Political Science Club, the Debate Club, Mathletes, and the Literary Club.

What we learned on-site:

* The clubs of interest would be appropriate, high-quality cocurricular activities for the prospective student. The clubs are very active and would welcome a new student.

* If a student is interested in a particular sport, the student is recommended to a coach or the athletic director to determine the student's eligibility. The student needs academic clearance to compete in a school sport.

Concluding summary:

The mature cocurricular activities available would complement the prospective student's academic course selections well. The cocurricular activities would further test the skills of the prospective student, providing an additional "stretch" beyond the classroom.

PARENT/COMMUNITY RELATIONS

What we learned from all the data provided:

* The Program Planning Guide begins with a Foreword to Parents that encourages parental involvement in the academic planning for the students. Several activities are scheduled for parents to provide assistance with the planning:

1. Discussion in classrooms of course offerings in each academic area.
2. Special presentations by teachers and department coordinators regarding specific courses and programs.
3. An evening meeting for parents to give an overview of the educational program at the high school.
4. Student conferences with counselors to discuss and select courses. (Counselors are also available to discuss course selection with parents at their request.)

What we wanted to learn during the visit:

Do parents take advantage of the counselors for academic discussions?

What we learned on-site:

* Parents do participate in academic course selection and are involved in key decisions as, for example, a decision about taking an AP course.
* Parents are informed when students are in academic difficulty.

Concluding summary:

The emphasis on parental participation with academic planning is clear from its prominence at the beginning of the Program Planning Guide. Parental involvement is very important for this highly talented student who has several optional career paths within the areas of interest given.

OVERALL SUMMARY FOR CASE STUDY 2

The prospective student would be well suited for the high academically achieving environment of Council Rock High School. Included in the wide range of course offerings are honors courses and college-level (AP) courses in all the areas of interest as well as the Gifted Program and the advanced distance learning mathematics course. Clubs and other activities are offered that are directly related to the student's areas of interest, providing a challenging extension of the classroom experience. The small class sizes will permit active student involvement in classes. The grounded, focused school environment speaks to the strong leadership of the school. Despite its size, a consistent academic focus and student-centered emphasis have been successfully maintained. This seems to us a remarkable achievement, given the recent rapid growth of Council Rock High School from one primarily for children of a small farm community to one that now serves children from a growing population of varied occupational and educational backgrounds.

Case Study 3
An Urban High School:
Bayonne High School
Bayonne, New Jersey

Student Description. The student we had in mind for this visit is of above average academic ability, with an interest in computers. This student is considering a career path in engineering as a computer scientist, but also has a strong art interest and wonders whether computer graphics may be the better direction to pursue. The student also has an interest in theater and writing.

Before the Visit. Two websites were examined prior to the visit: the state-created school report card and Bayonne High School's own website. The website for the school's report card provided data for three years so we were able to compare data and note consistencies (the most recent data given at this website is for the 1995–96 school year). We were also sent the following information prior to our visit: Bayonne High School Profile, Curriculum Offerings and Proficiencies, Student Information Booklet, a welcome booklet for eighth graders that outlines career pathways and ninth-grade course offerings, Course Selection lists by grade level, Advanced Placement course guide, and the publication of a workshop delivered by the principal, Dr. Michael A. Wanko, at the NASSP National Convention in February 2000 titled "Creating Safe and Supportive Schools—Prevention and Response."

The School Visit. Bayonne High School is located on a 13–acre waterfront campus within an urban setting. The neighborhood surrounding the school is densely populated (62,000 by the last census, an "undercount"). The city is comprised of two- to three-story structures, approximately 70 percent of which are two-family homes. The school district is classified by the state as District Factor B. [Factors range from the lowest economic level (A) to the highest economic level (J).] The city is 1 mile by 3 miles and adjacent to a major city. The main building of the campus is an architecturally handsome three-story gothic structure built in 1936. As the school has grown over the years, more contemporary architectural features have been added to the four-building campus. Dr. Wanko, the principal, has taken care to restore architectural features such as the leaded windows in the library, which display stained glass images of printers' symbols. One building on the campus is a shared school/community physical education structure that contains an NHL regulation ice rink, indoor track, dance studio, and two gymnasiums. The main buildings house a planetarium, special facilities for sciences and arts, an auditorium, three cafeterias, a vocational wing, driving simulators, indoor swimming pool, five other gyms, wrestling/martial arts room, and two facilities for nautilus, hydraulic, and free weight training.

We entered Bayonne High School through a hallway of flags representing each of the fifty countries that the current students are from. On duty at the main entrance were three permanent substitute teachers, assigned to security duty, who were prepared for our visit and welcomed us warmly.

ORGANIZATIONAL AND ADMINISTRATIVE VITALITY/EFFECTIVENESS

What we learned from all the data provided:

Bayonne High School's mission statement is: "Our mission is to provide students with quality educational programs and a safe and supportive learning environment enabling them to maximize their potential and become healthy, happy, productive and fulfilled citizens." An additional statement is in the school's profile: "Our school espouses the values of a solid work ethic, good citizenship and a sense of morality that supports the community's way of life. Students are encouraged to develop a sense of responsibility that enables them to be both self-disciplined and self-reliant, particularly in the areas of punctuality and attendance."

School Motto: "Faith, Honor, Determination."

Bayonne High School was selected:

* As a state finalist in the U.S. Department of Education's Blue Ribbon School Program.

* By the Department of Education for the Star School Award, one of the two finest high schools in the state.

* By the Department of Education for two Best Practice Awards:

1. For the High-Adventure course curriculum.
2. For educational support (Look at Me, See Within Program).

* By the state's monthly magazine as one of the state's 45 "great public high schools."

* Dr. Wanko has received numerous awards, including the state's Golden Lamp Award and the NASSP Principal of the Year Award.

* Bayonne High School is divided into six houses. Students are grouped heterogeneously in the same house for all of their four years. Each house has its own vice principal, guidance counselors, secretary, and assigned faculty members. The house organization supplies continuity and a "small-school" environment for the students while also providing the wide program and resource offering of a large institution.

* School Safety: A state-of-the-art security system exists. The Student Dress Code prohibits "gangwear"-style clothing and accessories.

+ Average Daily Attendance: 90.9 percent as compared with the state average of 92 percent.

+ Student/Administrator Ratio: 288:1, compared with the state average of 173:1.

+ Median Salary of Administrators: $73,110 as compared with the state average of $78,956.

* Years of Experience of Administrators: twenty-five (district) as compared with the state average of twenty-five.

* Student/Parent/Guardian Responsibilities are clearly stated in the Student Information Booklet. Both Bayonne High School and Board of Education Policies are included. The following policies are explained: School Attendance, School Safety, Smoke Free Campus rules, Substance Abuse Policy, Promotion Requirements, Commencement Requirements, Cutting Policy, Report Card Distribution dates, Dismissal Procedure, PM Detention, AM Detention, Entertainment Devices/Beepers, Tardiness to Class, Off Limit Areas, Hall Discipline, Family Life and Drug Alcohol Curriculum, Student Dress Code, Class Time Absence Policy, Sexual Harassment Policy, Equal Educational Opportunity Policy.

* Dr. Wanko recently delivered a workshop on school safety at a National Association of Secondary School Principals (NASSP) conference.

What we wanted to learn during the visit:

How exactly do you promote school safety?
How are the students selected for the houses?

What we learned on-site:

* Regarding School Safety: The security team is employed on a full-time basis so the team members are able to know the students. A Community Oriented Police Officer is available via a grant-funded program. The officers are members of the community police force. They are present in the cafeteria and also teach DARE classes; consequently they get to know the students in the classroom as well. Students have an ID card that is swiped for entrance into the school. A new metal detector (similar to an airport detector) is available for further security. In the cafeteria there are assigned seats to promote an orderly atmosphere (which is amazingly quiet!).

* Regarding the House System: To determine which house a new student should be placed in, the counselors in the elementary schools meet together with the counselors at Bayonne High School and make assignments to assure an even racial/ethnic mix and inclusion of all career orientations. Within the house the students remain in the same homeroom (from 9 to 35 minutes each morning) for all of their four years. Upperclassmen are available to each homeroom to give students the opportunity to ask questions of them. Each

house has a counselor and a vice principal permanently assigned to it to provide continuity. The students take courses in all facilities regardless of the house assignment. Grades and reports from all teachers are given to the vice principal of the house in which students are grouped.

* Dr. Wanko actively and successfully recruits students for Bayonne High School, which has several private school competitors.

* The Ambassador Program is made up of Dr. Wanko and a group of students who visit elementary schools to recruit students for Bayonne High School. Students who have graduated from each elementary school are available for these visits. The ambassadors wear a uniform of garnet-colored jackets adorned with the emblem of the school.

* Welcoming new students: On the first day of school the ambassadors are present in their uniforms. Other students also take part in new student orientation. A tour of the school is given by students and a meeting takes place with the house vice principal. They participate in student vignettes on high school adjustment. At this time there is a welcoming barbecue and recruitment by the student clubs.

* A Parent Night is held for the incoming ninth-grade students prior to their ninth-grade school year.

* Before attending the school a student (and a parent, if desired) could shadow a student throughout a day or attend classes of specific interest.

* The welcoming flags in the foyer of the school attest to the different cultural backgrounds. Students speak thirty-nine different "first" languages.

* Alumni frequently return to the school for events. A Hall of Fame featured prominently in the main hallway of the school honors former graduates who have earned a high level of prominence in their professions.

* There is active and creative fund-raising for the school. For example, the building has been rented out for various television events/productions (with the provision that the school's students be used for extras and that those performing in the productions agree to speak to the students in their classes). Speakers have included script writers in English classes, artisans and craft workers in art classes, construction workers in vocational shops, and cameramen in photography classes. With the funds earned from these rentals the school is able to obtain educational resources, such as computers for the library. Examples of funding from grant sources were frequently given during our visit.

The Board of Education is appointed by the mayor.

* Dr. Wanko described his management style as "MBWA" (Management by Walking Around). He walks at least 3 miles/day throughout the school and carries a walkie-talkie in order to be in instant contact with offices and other administrators throughout the building. In this way he is alert to the happenings of the school and his presence is visible to all school members.

* The facility and grounds are very well maintained and obviously respected.

Concluding summary:

The administrators exhibit extraordinary organizational and administrative vitality that results in a nearly seamless organization to the school. It is obvious that Dr. Wanko is an active, visible, knowledgeable, and powerful force in the school's everyday operations. We were impressed by his knowledge about the details of the curriculum. Dr. Wanko is obviously a person of action and not one to let any opportunity to advance Bayonne High School go by. As an example, he has used an entrepreneurial orientation to forge alliances with the community that have resulted in outstanding facilities. The organization of Bayonne High School is focused on the job of learning and it was evident to us that the expectations of the students were clear. The architectural design and well-maintained facilities promote this focus, too. The students take care of the property and seem to know that it is "their" school. We were impressed with the emphasis on providing a safe atmosphere and Dr. Wanko's proactive leadership in this area. Our prospective student would be well supported in the orderly and safe learning environment of the school.

INSTRUCTIONAL ENVIRONMENT (TEACHERS AND LEARNERS)

What we learned from all the data provided:

The size of the school is relatively large (2,170 students).

The student racial/ethnic makeup is diverse: White (63 percent), Hispanic (24 percent), Black (8 percent), Asian (5 percent). Thirty-nine different languages are spoken by the student population, including Arabic, Italian, Korean, Spanish, Polish and Filipino. The student population represents fifty different countries.

Nine hundred students qualify for the free breakfast and lunch program.

* Student/Faculty Ratio is average for the state: 12/1.

+ Faculty Academic Degrees: 39 percent have either a Master's or Doctoral Degree.

22 percent of the students are classified (eligible for an Individualized Educational Program).

* Average Class Size: 21 as compared with the state average of 20.6.

+ Student Mobility Rate: 13 percent of the students entered or left the school during the school year, compared with the state average of 14.4 percent.

* Faculty Attendance Rate: 96.4 percent, compared with the state average of 96.3 percent.

* Median Salary of Faculty: $50,575, compared with the state average of $50,025.

* Years of Experience of Faculty: fifteen (District) as compared with the state average of sixteen.

* Revenues: Local Taxes: 65 percent, as compared with the state average of 55 percent (This represents a strong local commitment to the school.). State Taxes: 27 percent, compared with the state average of 38 percent. Federal Taxes: 5 percent, compared with the state average of 3 percent. Other: 3 percent, compared with the state average of 4 percent.

^ Per Pupil Expenditures: $6,951, compared with the state average of $7,759. (This amount has steadily increased over a three-year period.)

What we wanted to learn during the visit:

What professional development opportunities exist for teachers?

What we learned on-site:

* The school environment is well ordered, with an exciting atmosphere.

* We were introduced to students, teachers, administrators, security officials, guidance staff, and other staff members throughout the day. Each spoke with an enthusiasm and commitment to the learning experience.

* Professional development opportunities are ongoing "in-house" throughout the year. Current educational issues are addressed and training offered.

* There is an astonishing amount of professional stability within the school. This was reinforced as we met numerous school professionals who had a long history in the community and with the school. Over half of the staff are graduates of Bayonne High School and the children of the staff residing in the city attend the school.

There are 400 students who quality for an IEP (Individualized Educational Program). These students are eligible to take courses at Bayonne High School until the age of twenty-two. Marketable skills are taught and students are given skills such as the ability to apply for a state driver's license.

* Teachers often participate with students in out-of-school programs (e.g., producing computer graphics for shows and contests and composing and performing music in major city performances).

* In the introduction we described the extensive facilities available to the students.

Concluding summary:

Our prospective student has diverse interests that can be addressed in this setting, which has a large selection of course offerings and learning experiences (discussed in detail in the next sections "Richness of the Curriculum" and "Student Life"). A diverse student population is recognized as an excellent preparation for the workplace and this multicultural setting will well prepare our student for both college and potential workplace settings. Although the school size is large, the house organization promotes a "small-school" environment with the opportunities of a large school. The small class size gives an opportunity for faculty–student interaction. And the stability of the professional staff would be an asset for any student. Although the per pupil expenditures are lower than the state's average, there are excellent resources, some obtained by grants, entrepreneurial efforts, and business contributions (as discussed in the sections "Organizational and Administrative Vitality/Effectiveness" and "Parent/Community Relations"). Our student's chosen career paths would all be well supported by the school's facilities and resources.

RICHNESS OF THE CURRICULUM

What we learned from all the data provided:

* The four-year comprehensive high school offers both academic and career preparation programs with more than 300 course offerings. Distance learning allows the school to offer additional courses. The course descriptions are particularly useful, providing both a description of the course and the expected proficiencies. Honors Programs are available for all the academic areas, with the English and Social Studies programs cited as "exceptional" by a major university. College-level courses are offered through cooperation with nearby colleges, providing the opportunity to earn up to twenty-one college credits in areas such as Calculus, Physics, Chemistry, U.S. History, and American Government. Students are prepared to take Advanced Placement tests in Art History, English, World Languages, Mathematics, Sciences, and Social Studies.

* Language Arts: The course descriptions are striking with their consistent references to the integration of reading, interpreting, evaluating, writing, and speaking. The emphasis on library research skills and the requirements for research papers are also remarkable. All the National Council of Teachers of English (NCTE) Standards are reflected in these descriptions. Students are exposed to a wide range of texts and a wide range of literatures (including biographies, world myths, folktales, Greek and Roman literature, literature of the Middle Ages, Shakespeare, Renaissance, literature of the nineteenth and twentieth centuries). Language Arts are integrated with two other areas of the curriculum (World Cultures and U.S. History I) to promote conceptual thinking for honors students. A unique offering is the Analytical Reading and Reasoning course designed to better prepare students for the SAT, with emphases on vocabulary development, better understanding of verbal questions, and the use of logical thought.

* Mathematics: Several academic levels are addressed with the mathematics curriculum: general, college preparatory, college level, honors, and AP Calculus. In particular, we noted references to the following National Council of Teachers of Mathematics (NCTM) Standards: problem solving and reasoning and proof. Several courses are designed with "real-life" applications.

* Social Studies: This is a particularly rich social studies curriculum that includes a 20-hour service learning requirement. All the National Council for the Social Studies (NCSS) Standards are met including an examination of the impact of technology on our society. Examination, interpretation, and understanding are woven into each course. Some highlights of the curriculum: world religious influences; the emphasis on evaluating information from a variety of resources (primary and secondary sources, maps, charts, graphs, tables); relating current events to past history; the influence of geography; a Political/Legal Education course that interprets and analyzes court cases; an American Social Issues course that examines Family Issues in American Life, The Impact of Technology, The Impact of Sports in American Life, Violence in American Life, and We the People.

* Science: Many of the National Science Education Standards (NSES) are met with an emphasis throughout the curriculum on scientific inquiry. Unique course offerings include Environmental Science, Ecology/Marine Science, Science Seminar (where some students are encouraged to compete in the county science fair), Astronomy, an Advanced Computers course (including C programming language) and Pascal Programming.

* The Arts: The Art and Music program is particularly rich. Vocal music opportunities include award winning vocal music groups such as a Men's Chorus, a Concert Choir, a Girls Glee Club, the Madrigals, and the Metropolitan Opera Workshop. Instrumental music opportunities include a Jazz Ensemble, String Ensemble, Brass Ensemble, Electronic Music, and Concert and Marching Bands. Other music opportunities include: Harmony, Music History, Theory and Fundamentals of Music. Theater opportunities exist in the Language Arts curriculum (Foundations of Theatre Arts, Advanced Theatre Arts, Independent Theatre Arts, and Shakespeare). Visual arts opportunities include courses such as Art History, Electronic Commercial Art, Ceramics, Arts and Crafts, Photography, Studio Art, Art I and II, Computer Graphics and Sculpture. This is an exemplary art and music curriculum. Students have a broad opportunity to learn to communicate "their thoughts and feelings in a variety of modes, giving them a vastly more powerful repertoire of self-expression" (National Standards for Arts Education, NSAE). Among the proficiencies expected are the following, all in keeping with the NSAE Standards: To develop a personal power of expression; to develop a feeling of self-worth, while enriching the students' aesthetic and practical life through the art experience; to enable a student to express, intensify, and clarify his or her ideas and feelings through the use of the fundamental elements of art; to display art literacy (through increased: knowledge of artists, their styles, periods and works; art vocabulary, applied creative thinking skills; and ability to articulate critiques of artwork). An Arts Seminar is available to Honors Students. Independent Studies are available for an entire year for both art and music.

* Information Literacy: Research skill development is highly integrated throughout the curriculum with all the information literacy elements proposed by the American Association of School Librarians (AASL) included.

* Foreign Language: In addition to offering four years of Spanish, Italian, French, Latin, and German, students may take three years of Japanese and two years of Polish. A Conversational Spanish course and a Conversational Italian course are also offered.

* English as a Second Language (ESL): This program is integrated throughout the curriculum.

* Transition to work programs: The vocational program offers training in hands-on occupations such as building trades and welding (gas and electric). Specific courses include: Industrial Technology I & II, Shop, Introduction to Vocational Trades. Business Education courses include: Retailing Work Study, Accounting I, II & CP (college prep), Bookkeeping I & II, Cooperative Business Education (work/study program), Marketing Education Lab, General Marketing, Marketing Work/Study, Introduction to Business Vocations, Principles of Business, Orientation to Work, Keyboarding I & II, Desktop Publishing Applications, Data Management Application, Television Production. The Television Production Studio allows the school to offer courses in video journalism and television production. Vocational/Technical courses are offered both in Bayonne High School and at a nearby school of technology.

* Moral Education: A unique offering to grades 11 and 12 is the Peer Leadership program designed as a support system for incoming grade 9 students. Topics that these upperclassmen cover to assist the younger students are: improvement of self-esteem, increased awareness of self and others, improved relationship with others, communication skills, listening skills, and decision making. These are important ingredients for one to learn to "respect human dignity" and "care about the welfare of others" (ASCD Panel on Moral Education). The service learning requirement should assist students with their integration of "individual interests and social responsibilities" (ASCD). These are valuable examples of the integration of moral education within the curriculum.

* Eighteen career pathways are offered based on the region's demographics and employment patterns. These include: Agriculture Production, Forestry and Fishing; Construction; Manufacturing, Installation and Repair; Utilities, Environmental and Waste Management; Transportation; Telecommunications, Computers, Arts, Entertainment and Information; Wholesale/Retail Sales, Real Estate and Personnel Services; Restaurants, Lodging, Hospitality and Tourism, Amusement/Recreation; Finance and Insurance; Health and Human Services; Education and Training; Business and Administration Services; Scientific and Technical Services.

What we wanted to learn during the visit:

What are the examples of and advantages of distance learning provided by the school?

How is technology integrated into the curriculum?

Are the students involved in curriculum design?

What efforts are made and what opportunities exist for low achieving students?

What we learned on-site:

A committee of seven professionals coordinates the core curriculum of Bayonne High School.

* The expertise and commitment of the staff was obvious to us, in particular, from the detailed curriculum discussions that we had with several of the professional staff members.

* Student involvement in the curriculum includes recommending the school's annual theme to Dr. Wanko, who selects from the student recommendations. This year's theme centers on understanding of others.

* There is an emphasis on accurate academic placement during course selection since changes can only be made annually.

* For additional vocational training, in addition to the wide range of training available on site, students from the junior level are transported to a technical school 30 minutes away.

* Distance Learning is used to supplement the vast range of course offerings. For example, a nearby high school can offer Japanese to both its students and the students of Bayonne High School, while Bayonne High School can offer German to both institutions. This takes advantage of two faculty strengths at two different institutions.

* We were exposed to several examples of the use of instructional technology within the curriculum. There is a stock market program that introduces students to tracking and trading stocks utilizing websites. The graphic arts computer lab allows students to perform at a professional level.

* The Art and Music program is highly integrated into the curriculum and open to all students. A list of eighth graders with arts potential is given to the Art/Music Director and letters are sent to the parents of each of these students describing the Art and Music program, including a list of classes available, and inviting the student to a performance. The list of students is given to both art and music teachers and counselors at Bayonne High School. Students are asked to bring the letter with them to the guidance counselor prior to course selection. We spoke with the Art/Music Director (i.e., coordinator) of the district (pre-kindergarten through grade 12). The Director has worked in the district for thirty years and served for sixteen years in the current position. Dr. Wanko is a very strong advocate for the Art and Music program. The number of performances and presentations (art and music) continues to increase dra-

matically. One annual art exhibit is a faculty, student, alumni art exhibit. Art and music provide natural links to other aspects of the curriculum, including the history (e.g., biographies of composers), science (e.g., musical vibrations), literature, and computer programs. Further interrelationships between social studies and the arts were discussed at a recent workshop. For honors students offerings include an Honors Art Seminar, with an emphasis on seeing the humanities through the eyes of artists, and an Art Portfolio program. There is a partnership with the state's symphony orchestra. There is a rental program for instruments and donations to the program are used to purchase instruments.

* We observed a class in the school library media center that was being conducted by the school library media center specialist in conjunction with a subject course, thus integrating the information skills into a curricular area rather than teaching the skills in isolation.

* Special Education programs include the Culinary Arts Program with an emphasis on learning job skills for the culinary arts profession.

* The High Adventure program promotes team building and physical challenge.

* The television studio housed in the school works in conjunction with the city's educational television network. Some of the programs initiated at Bayonne High School include study guides for an academic game show, information about the current census process, and interviews with a congressperson. Public domain programming, such as NASA programs, is used where appropriate in the curriculum. Students from all the grades are encouraged to be involved with the studio, thus enabling the station to be a strong community asset.

* Typical courses and cocurricular activities (discussed in the section "Student Life") recommended by the Director of Student Personnel Services for the prospective student would include: three years of theater arts, all the computer courses within the business program, three computer courses within the science program, computer courses within the commercial art program, the theater group that performs in the fall and the spring, the Arts Seminar (a course that is taught with computer software developed at a nearby university), creative writing, Shakespeare, poetry, and the school's newspaper.

* Students may complete college-level courses and earn college credits through a program coordinated with a local college.

* To support students who require academic assistance tutors are available before school opens for English, Mathematics, Social Studies, and Science. The National Honor Society students also provide tutoring assistance.

Concluding summary:

The profile of our prospective student matches well with the opportunities offered by this high school. Specifically, as mentioned in the course selections above, the student would be able to choose from among the following: the rich Art and Music program (which includes Computer Graphics and Electronic Commercial Art), computer courses offered within the science curriculum (Advanced Computers and Pascal Programming), additional computer courses within the Business Education program, theater offerings (three years of Theatre Arts), and multiple writing opportunities within the Language Arts curriculum. Our student would be academically challenged and would find an especially broad course of studies to find a path to college and a career.

ACADEMIC ACHIEVEMENT

What we learned from all the data provided:

* Scholarship winners have included: National Merit Scholar, National Hispanic Scholar, National Achievement Scholar Semi-Finalist, National Merit Scholar Commended Student, Distinguished Scholars (a state award), Urban Scholars (a state award), State Governor's School Awards, Congressional District winners in the "We the People" Competition, County Championships in the Mock Trial Competition.

* Scholastic Assessment Test results: Of the top 25 percent of the Class of 1999: Math (average score) = 520 and Verbal (average score) = 530. Five students in the Class of 1999 achieved a perfect score on one or more sections of SAT 1 or SAT 2. Earlier results (1995–96) (all students): Math (average score) = 456, compared with the state average of 508. Verbal = 458 as compared with the state average of 496.

* Percentage of students taking the SAT: 78 percent, compared with the state average of 75 percent. (This number has increased considerably over a three-year period.)

* Advanced Placement Tests were given in Psychology, English Literature & Composition, Biology, Mathematics-Calculus AB, English Language & Composition.

* Vocal music groups are award winners.

* Theater students have been recognized by a local playhouse as "rising stars."

* Commercial Art and Photography students have been the recipients of many prestigious awards.

* Graduation Rate: 98.7 percent, compared with the state average of 98.9 percent. (This is not a four-year "graduation rate" for this class.)

* Percentage of students enrolled in four-year colleges: 77 percent of the College Prep Students and 58 percent of all students.

* Percentage of students enrolled in two-year colleges: 10 percent of the College Prep Students and 15 percent of all students.

* Percentage of students enrolled in Trade/Technical/Bus/Other: 3 percent of the College Prep Students and 14 percent of all students.

* High School Proficiency Test—Grade 11: (Percentage of students passing each section: reading, mathematics, writing, and the overall HSPT) Reading: 85.6 percent, compared with the state average of 83.4 percent.

Mathematics: 85.7 percent, compared with the state average of 86.2 percent. Writing: 94.8 percent, compared with the state average of 90.4 percent. All sections: 77.2 percent, compared with the state average of 75.6 percent.

* The school's Academic Bowl Team has won seven county championships during the past ten years and is currently ranked fifth in the state.

* Some of the colleges and universities that students currently attend include: Columbia University, Princeton University, Johns Hopkins University, Pennsylvania State University, Georgetown University, University of Chicago, Boston University, University of Notre Dame, Brown University.

What we wanted to learn during the visit as a follow-up to the pre-visit study:

How is excellence recognized?

What we learned on-site:

* Bayonne High School's Renaissance Program recognizes student excellence and effort at the end of each marking period. Renaissance cards are awarded to those students who have achieved academic excellence and have no discipline reports, no detentions, no failures, and good attendance in compliance with the school attendance policy. Students receive a Gold Card for grades of 90 average or above, a Garnet Card for grades of 80 average to 89 average, or a White Card for grades of 75 average to 79 average. The cards entitle the student to discounts provided by community businesses.

Concluding summary:

Bayonne High School is success-oriented and encourages excellence by recognition. Our prospective student would be in an academically challenging environment with the encouragement to embrace challenges beyond the immediate school environment. As noted in both this section and earlier sections, the school has received a plethora of awards, including the area of commercial art. As mentioned in the section "Instructional Environment," students participate regularly in computer graphics contests outside the school environment. This type of promotion of the students' abilities allows them to test their academic skills in "real-life" settings.

SUPPORT FOR LEARNING

What we learned from all the data provided:

* Counselor–student ratio: 1:217. (These ten counselors are located in the Guidance Center and primarily confer with students about academic decisions

such as course selection, schedules, and choices. They help students deal with difficulties that interfere with academic success. They also address social concerns of the students. Counselors are involved in college and career transitions and selection.)

* An additional five counselors are available in the Student Center to address a wide variety of student concerns.

* All classrooms have internet connections.

* The level of technology in the science labs and the library have placed the school in the top twenty-five of the state's school districts for technology.

* The School Student Center was awarded the Phi Delta Kappa Award for Outstanding Program.

What we wanted to learn during the visit:

We were a bit confused by the roles of the different guidance counselors and asked to have that clarified.

What we learned on-site:

* Regarding the counselors: there are ten guidance counselors in the Guidance Center who are primarily involved with academics including course selection, but also address social concerns of the students. There is also a grant-funded Student Center with five personnel (a school psychologist, two social workers, a guidance counselor, and a grant administrator). One of the activities of the Student Center personnel is to conduct group counseling sessions on topics of particular relevance to the current student population. The Director of Student Personnel Services oversees both programs in addition to nine elementary school counselors. There is strong communication between the elementary school and high school counselors to make the proper academic placement and provide a smooth transition to high school. Teacher recommendations play a strong role as well.

* An on-site planetarium (built in 1965) supports the science program. There are only four such facilities in high schools in the state.

Concluding summary:

The strong counseling program supports Bayonne High School students both academically and emotionally, certainly an asset for any student. Because our prospective student has two potential career paths in mind it will be essential for the student to work closely with the academic guidance counselors and we had great confidence in this counseling opportunity for the student. The high level of technological support available in the school is a "must" for our prospective student whose potential career directions depend on advanced computer technology.

STUDENT LIFE

What we learned from all the data provided:

* Nearly fifty-nine organizations are open to student participation.

* The Peer Leadership Program has over 100 students participating. This program concentrates on conflict mediation and resolution skills, improving communication, and after-school tutoring. The program includes a residential weekend program.

* More than 100 students participate in: Adopt a Homeroom, ERASE, SPHERE, and the ambassador program.

* The student newspaper is available both in print and electronic formats and has received the bronze medal by the Columbia Scholastic Press Association.

* The school's Literary Art Magazine was awarded a silver medal by the Columbia Scholastic Press Association and was awarded second prize by the American Scholastic Press Association.

* Athletic Program: Over fifty-five teams, including new varsity teams in wrestling, golf and fencing, are available in the fall, winter, and spring seasons. The teams have won four state and one national championships.

* The Class of 1999 earned eight county championships again this year.

* Dropout Rate: 3.6 percent (no state comparison is given here). This is relatively low.

What we wanted to learn during the visit:

Because the school's student population is large, is it possible for all students to participate in a cocurricular activity?

What we learned on-site:

* Theater: There are two performances each year (a comedy or drama in the fall and a musical in the spring). A summer performance is also given and open to all students in the community. A local playhouse has cited the performances as exemplary for the past four years. The drama students practice every evening for three hours. The students are also active in the community's teen center, addressing issues through drama.

* An Okinawan version of karate, Isshinryu, is available to the students. Japanese is the language used during the practice sessions.

* Mock Trial is available to Sophomores through Seniors and for all academic levels. Many of the practice and competitive sessions take place on Saturdays.

* The guidance and arts programs have worked together to form after school programs, some of which are grant-funded. These programs, which provide an opportunity to be expressive, are available to all students. One student shared his performance with us that dealt with racial diversity.

* A Travel Club exists that does include a student exchange program and some free trips.
* The athletic facilities are outstanding. In addition to the physical education structure and the athletic facilities described in the introduction there is a football stadium. A recent donation of materials for docks will provide the initial support for a future crew team.

Concluding summary:

Bayonne High School provides an amazing array of activities for students and allows for student input into the development of activities. As stated more than once, the activities are available to all students. Because the theater activities are year-round, our prospective student would have ample opportunity to pursue that interest. Our student's writing interest could be met further by involvement with the student newspaper or the Literary Art Magazine.

PARENT/COMMUNITY RELATIONS

What we learned from all the data provided:

* The Student Information Booklet outlines the school's policies, which are listed as "Student/Parent/Guardian Responsibilities." Policies included are: Absence, School Safety, Smoking, Substance Abuse, Promotion Requirements, Discipline, Student Dress Code, Sexual Harassment, and Equal Educational Opportunity.
* In the "Curriculum Offerings and Proficiencies" booklet, the "Fundamental Responsibilities of Parents and Guardians" are listed at the beginning.

What we wanted to learn during the visit:

What opportunities are there for the community to use the facilities?
What relationships exist between the school and the community?

What we learned on-site:

+ Parents receive progress reports throughout the year. The reports include up to five comments/course. At the end of the second marking period parents are informed if a student is failing a course. The parent may request a meeting with school personnel at this time.
* There is an ice skating rink that was built cooperatively with school funding and state funding (42 percent was paid by the state). Bayonne High School's contribution was made in response to a Middle State's recommendation that there be more physical fitness opportunities available for the students. Bayonne High School uses the facility between 6 A.M. and 5 P.M. and the facility is available to the community the rest of the time. The ice skating rink

can be rented for parties and proceeds from the rental support needs of the school.

   * Local businesses participate in an Adopt-the-School program.

   * There is a summer evening program conducted at Bayonne High School that was coordinated with the community with the intent of keeping the students occupied appropriately during the summer evening hours.

   * A promotional video has been created by Bayonne High School that is aired over the community's educational television network. The video won a state award in communication. Some of its highlights include: the school's many award-winning teachers, the concept that one never stops learning or growing, the rich academic atmosphere, the social values learned and their importance to a teenager's life, peer mediation programs, community service, the solid work ethic that is promoted, morality training, and the many cocurricular activities.

   * A promotional video, *Talk to Me,* has been created by Bayonne High School and aired over the community's educational television network. The video is addressed at assisting the social development of students by encouraging contact with other school community members. People who appear in the video include peer leaders, vice principals, the principal, guidance counselors, and the members of the Student Self-Advocacy Team.

   * Local businesses offer support in many ways. Some machines for one of the physical fitness centers were donated by a local business, for example.

   * Promotional newspaper coverage of the school is frequent which speaks to strong community support of the school.

Concluding summary:

Bayonne High School is an outstanding example of school–community cooperation and outreach. The many examples of community support for facility and resource development demonstrate the excellent relationship between the school and its community and it was obvious to us that the school is considered an integral part of the community. The school's skillful management of its outstanding facilities makes opportunities available for both students and members of the community. Thus, our prospective student would find multiple resources and opportunities available in the school due to the supportive school-community relationship.

OVERALL SUMMARY FOR CASE STUDY 3

The indicators of excellence found in the data provided prior to the on-site visit were supported and confirmed by the visit to Bayonne High School. Dr. Wanko and others we spoke with during the day consistently expressed that we had come to just the right school for our prospective student. The expressions of the students, staff, faculty, and administrators matched our own observations and impressions. Although one might be concerned that a student could "get lost" in a such a large school, the house organization actually provides a "small-school" atmosphere with exceptional professional support. This urban school can and does offer a multiple of academic and cocurricular choices, including all the desired choices of the prospective student's. The outstanding organizational and administrative vitality keeps the school in the forefront, promoting a challenging atmosphere with excellent resource support. The school is true to its mission of providing "quality educational programs" in a "safe and supportive learning environment." Students are encouraged to "maximize their potential" through programs such as the Renaissance Program, entering contests, and through the many cocurricular offerings. As we examined the information provided before the visit and our own observations made during the visit, it became clear that this school would be one that could fulfill all the interests and expectations of the prospective student.

Effective Education Categories (including data elements)

1—ORGANIZATIONAL AND ADMINISTRATIVE VITALITY/EFFECTIVENESS

Mission statement
Average daily attendance
Average daily membership
Number of students suspended or expelled
School climate
School safety

2—INSTRUCTIONAL ENVIRONMENT (TEACHERS AND LEARNERS)

Classroom

School enrollment
Class size
Student teacher ratio
Student mobility rate/enrollment stability
Expenditures
Ethnicity of the student body
Building age

Teacher

Average years teaching experience
Teacher salaries
Teacher education (degrees)
Professional development activities

Learner

Average daily attendance
(More about this is covered in sections: Academic Achievement and Student Life)

3—RICHNESS OF THE CURRICULUM

Curriculum offerings
Honors course offerings
Advanced Placement (AP) course offerings
School Library Media Center

4—ACADEMIC ACHIEVEMENT

Achievement test scores (standardized tests developed at the district, state, or national level)
Percentage of students taking the SAT or ACT
Percentage of graduates enrolled in two-year or four-year colleges
Subjects in which Advanced Placement Program courses are offered

5—SUPPORT FOR LEARNING

Instructional Resources (textbooks, science laboratory equipment, athletic equipment)
Technology Resources (e.g., number of students/computer)
Counselor-student ratio
Aide-to-teacher ratio

6—STUDENT LIFE

Cocurricular activities
Dropout rate

7—PARENT/COMMUNITY RELATIONS

PTA/PTO information
Volunteer information
Involvement of community organizations
Level of involvement expected by the school

7—PARENT/COMMUNITY RELATIONS

APPENDIX B

Data Sources (for demographic and education information)

LOCATING DEMOGRAPHIC INFORMATION

Data Sources (for demographic and education information)

LOCATING DEMOGRAPHIC INFORMATION

Chambers of Commerce

Johnson's world wide chamber of commerce directory. Annual. Loveland, CO: Johnson
   Publishing Co., 1983– .
Chamber of Commerce Listings available at: Http://www.town-usa.com/chambers/
   chamberlist.html.
United States Metropolitan areas via Yahoo (includes community information, e.g.,
   cultures and groups, government, organizations) available at: Http://dir.ya-
   hoo.com/regional/u_s_metros.
United States Census Bureau (U.S. Dept. of Commerce) available at: Http://
   www.census.gov.
County and City Databook. Annual. (Supplements the *Statistical Abstract of the
   United States*).

LOCATING EDUCATION INFORMATION

State Departments of Education available at: Http://www.asd.com/asd/
   edconn/tr-doe.htm.
National Center for Education Statistics (NCES) available at: Http://nces.ed gov.
   (NCES is the primary federal entity for collecting and analyzing data that are
   related to education in the United States and other nations.)

Several key publications of NCES:

The Condition of Education. Annual.

Digest of Education Statistics. Annual.
Projections of Education Statistics. Annual.
Learning about Education through Statistics. (1996).
State Indicators in Education 1997.

State comparisons of education statistics: 1969–70 to 1996–97. (Snyder, T. D. & Hoffman, C. M., 1998).
Common Core of Data (CCD) available at: Http:// nces.ed.gov/ccd. (The *Common Core of Data*, a program of the U.S. Department of Education's National Center for Education Statistics, is a comprehensive, annual, national statistical database of information concerning all public elementary and secondary schools—approximately 87,000—and school districts—approximately 16,000.)
Schools and Staffing Survey (SASS) available at: Http://nces.ed.gov/surveys/SASS/. (The *Schools and Staffing Survey* is the nation's largest sample survey of the characteristics and conditions of America's public and private schools and the teachers and principals who work in them. Conducted by the National Center for Education Statistics, SASS offers a source of data for policymakers, educators, educational researchers, and the general public.)
The Nation's Report Card/National Assessment of Educational Progress (NAEP) available at: Http://nces.ed.gov/nationsreportcard/site/home.asp.
Key publications of NAEP available at: Http://nces.ed.gov/pubsearch/ getpubcats.asp?sid=031.
Report cards for: writing, science, reading, arts, civics, geography, mathematics, and history.

National Standards

Language Arts

National Council of Teachers of English: The list of standards for the English language arts available at: Http://ncte.org/standards/thelist.html.

Mathematics

NCTM: *Principles & standards for school mathematics* available at: Http://www. nctm.org/standards.

Social Studies

Standards & position statements available at: Http://www.ncss.org/standards/home.html.

Science

National science education standards available at: Http://books.nap.edu/html/nses.

The Arts

National standards for arts education available at: Http://artsedge.kennedy-center.org/forms/arts1.html.

Additional information may be obtained from: MENC—The National Association for Music Education, 1806 Robert Fulton Drive, Reston, VA 20191 (phone: 800–336–3768)

See also: National Endowment for the Arts: NEA available at: Http://www.arts.endow.gov/partner.

Information Literacy

AASL Position Statements available at: Http://www.ala.org/aasl/positions/index.html.

Foreign Language

Standards for Foreign Language Learning available at: Http://www.actfl.org/htdocs/standards/standards.htm.

School Counseling

National Standards for School Counseling Programs of the American School Counselor Association (ASCA) available at: Http://www.schoolcounselor.org/national.htm.

Other Education Sources

The College Board (source for SAT information) available at: Http://www.collegeboard.org.

Blue Ribbon Winners available at: Http://www.ed.gov/offices/OERI/BlueRibbon Schools/frames/states.html.

Tips from Counselors: Recommended Preparation When Transferring to a New School

- Be sure to bring with you to the new school all information related to the prior school:
    All school records
    Report cards
    Transcript
    Course descriptions from the prior school
    Course selection sheets from the prior school
    Program Planning Guide from the prior school
    School Profile of the prior school
    Grading scale of the prior school

- Also bring with you to the new school:
    Four proofs of residency
    Proof of all immunizations

- The student should be prepared to be tested for proper placement in the new school. For some transfers between different states, students may have to be evaluated in order to transfer to an AP or Honors class. If your child is in a school that has intensive scheduling, it is very difficult for that student to transfer schools in the middle of the academic year, particularly if the school transferred to does not use intensive scheduling.

- When a student has transferred, the guidance counselor will ask the student about his or her previous school and the student's particular needs in the new school.

Be candid about:

The student's past difficulties (a principal also emphasized this). The new school will be able to help your child much more effectively if the school has all the facts about the student.

Special education needs.

Your financial situation if the student will need assistance. Among the many types of assistance available, food assistance is included.

Be sure to ask:

What types of colleges are students from the new high school attending?

How many National Merit Finalists, Semi-Finalists, and Commendations have been named from the school? Where do these students attend college?

What are typical AP scores and SAT scores? What does the school do to help the students in their preparation for standardized tests?

What are the testing programs for basic skills and state assessments? How does the school fare?

How is weighting and class ranking determined? Some schools may have an unweighted GPA; some may use only the majors from the previous school for weighting. This is important for competitive schools.

How many literature classes does the new school have? Are there enough to satisfy the student's curiosity?

Will my child know who the administrators are?

If the student has an athletic interest, ask to see the coach or the athletic director to determine eligibility for the particular sport(s) in the new school.

Bibliography

AASL Position Statements. American Association of School Librarians, American Library Association [Online]. Available: Http://www.ala.org/aasl/positions/index.html [1999].

Aiken, W. M. (1942). *Adventures in American education: Vol. 1. The story of the eight-year study.* New York: HarperCollins.

Angus, D. L. & Mirel, J. E. (1999). *The failed promise of the American high school, 1890–1995.* New York: Teachers College Press.

ASCD Panel on Moral Education (May 1988). Moral education in the life of the school. *Educational Leadership, 45* (9), 4–8. Reprinted with permission from the Association for Supervision and Curriculum Development (ASCD). All rights reserved.

Baker, E. L. (1988). Can we fairly measure the quality of education? *NEA Today, 6* (6), 9–14.

Bass, S. (1997). *The school report.* Stamford, CT: National School Reporting Services.

Bobbitt, S., Quinn, P., & Dabbs, P. (1992). *Filling the gaps: An overview of data on education in grades K through 12.* Washington, DC: U.S. Department of Education, Office of Educational Research and Improvement, National Center for Education Statistics.

Boyd, J. P., (Ed.). (1950). *The papers of Thomas Jefferson: Volume I: 1760 to 1766.* Princeton, NJ: Princeton University Press.

Boyer, E. L. (1983). *High school: A report on secondary education in America.* New York: Harper & Row.

Boyer, E. L. (1995). *The basic school.* Princeton, NJ: The Carnegie Foundation.

Breaking ranks: Changing an American institution (1996). Reston, VA: National Association of Secondary School Principals.

Buechler, M. (1996). *Charter schools: Legislation and results after four years.* Bloomington: Indiana Educational Policy Center.

Button, H. W. & Provenzo, E. F., Jr. (1983). *History of education and culture in America*. Englewood Cliffs, NJ: Prentice-Hall.

Coalition of Essential Schools. (2000). *Ten common principles* [Online]. Available: Http://www.essentialschools.org/aboutus/phil/10cps.html

Coleman, J. S. et al. (1966). *Equality of educational opportunity*. Washington, DC: U.S. Government Printing Office.

College Entrance Examination Board. (1983). *Academic preparation for college*. New York: The College Board.

Commission on the Reorganization of Secondary Education (1918). *Cardinal principles of secondary education*. Bureau of Education Bulletin, no. 35. Washington, DC: U.S. Government Printing Office.

Conant, J. B. (1959). *The American high school today*. New York: McGraw-Hill.

Conant, J. B. (1967). *The comprehensive high school: A second report to interested citizens*. New York: McGraw-Hill.

The condition of education (1999, Annual). Washington, DC: U.S. Department of Education, Office of Educational Research and Improvement, National Center for Education Statistics.

Coney, F., III. (1991, April). *Promoting school improvement practices: Developing quality effective school assessment indicators*. Paper presented at the Annual Meeting of the American Educational Research Association, Chicago, IL (ERIC Document Reproduction Service No. ED 332 336).

Corcoran, T. B. & Wilson, B. L. (1985). *The secondary school recognition program: A first report of 202 high schools*. Philadelphia, PA: Research for Better Schools, Inc.

Corcoran, T. B. & Wilson, B. L. (1986). *The search for successful secondary schools: The first three years of the secondary school recognition program*. Philadelphia, PA: Research for Better Schools, Inc.

Cremin, L. A. (1980). *American education: The national experience 1783–1876*. New York: Harper & Row.

Darling-Hammond, L. (1997). *The right to learn*. San Francisco, CA: Jossey-Bass.

Derived information related to groups of students. (Date NA). National Center for Education Statistics [Online]. Available: Http://nces.ed.gov/pubs2000/studenthb/append_D.asp [June 10, 2000].

Digest of education statistics. (1998, Annual). Washington, DC: U.S. Department of Education, Office of Educational Research and Improvement, National Center for Education Statistics.

Dropout rate. (2000). National Center for Education Statistics [Online]. Available: Http://nces.ed.gov/ssbr/pages/dropout.asp [June 10, 2000].

Ediger, M. (1988). *How should student achievement be determined?* Research report. Illinois: N.A. (ERIC Document Reproduction Service No. ED 301 582).

Edmonds, R. R. (1979). Effective schools for the urban poor. *Educational Leadership* 37(10), 15–24.

Firestone, W. A., Herriott, R., & Wilson, B. (1984). *Explaining the differences between elementary and secondary schools: Individual, organizational, and institutional perspectives*. Philadelphia: Research for Better Schools, Inc.

Fox, R. S. et al. (1974). *School climate improvement: A challenge to the school administrator*. Bloomington, IN: Phi Delta Kappa.

Frederick, J. M. (1987). *Measuring school effectiveness: Guidelines for educational practitioners.* Washington, DC: Office of Educational Research and Improvement. (ERIC Document Reproduction Service No. ED 282 891).

Gable, R. et al. (1986). *The development of the pilot form of the parent attitudes toward school effectiveness (PATSE) questionnaire.* A paper presented at the annual meeting of the National Counsel on Measurement in Education, San Francisco, CA, April 1, 1986. (ERIC Document Reproduction Service No. ED 277 733).

Gardner, H. (1983). *Frames of mind: The theory of multiple intelligences.* New York: Basic Books.

George, P. S., McEwin, C. K. & Jenkins, J. M. (2000). *The exemplary high school.* New York: Harcourt.

Gerald, D. E. & Hussar, W. J. (1998). *Projections of education statistics to 2008.* Washington, DC: National Center for Education Statistics.

Good, T. L. & Brophy, J. E. (1991). *Looking in classrooms.* New York: HarperCollins.

Goodlad, J. I. (1984). *A place called school: Prospects for the future.* New York: McGraw-Hill.

Grant, G. (1988). *The world we created at Hamilton High.* Cambridge, MA: Harvard University Press.

Harrison, C. (1991). *Public schools U.S.A.: A comparative guide to school districts.* New York: R. R. Bowker.

Information literacy: A position paper on information problem solving. American Association of School Librarians, American Library Association, Wisconsin Educational Media Association [Online]. Available: Http://www.ala.org/aasl/positions/ps_infolit.html [June 13, 2000]. Extracts reprinted with permission from AASL, ALA.

Internet access in public schools and classrooms: 1994–98. (February, 1999). National Center for Education Statistics [Online]. Available: Http://nces.ed.gov/pubs99/1999017.html [June 10, 2000].

Johnson, J. A. et al. (Eds.) (1991). *Introduction to the foundations of education* (Annotated instructor's edition). Boston: Allyn and Bacon.

Keefe, J. W. & Howard, E. R. (1997). *Redesigning schools for the new century: A systems approach.* Reston, VA: National Association of Secondary School Principals.

Kozol, J. (1991). *Savage inequalities: Children in America's schools.* New York: Crown Publishers, Inc.

Krug, E. A. (1964). *The shaping of the American high school.* New York: Harper & Row.

Krug, S. E. (1993). *Monitoring the "health" of the school. Project report.* Urbana, IL: National Center for School Leadership. (ERIC Document Reproduction Service No. ED 363 963).

Learning about education through statistics. (1996). Washington, DC: U.S. Department of Education, Office of Educational Research and Improvement, National Center for Education Statistics.

Lewis, L. et al. (Spring 1999). Teacher quality: A report on the preparation and qualifications of public school teachers. *Educational Statistics Quarterly, 1* (1), 7–11.

Lightfoot, S. L. (1983). *The good high school.* New York: Basic Books.

Loomis, A. K., Lide, E. S., & Johnson, B. L. (1933). *The program of studies*. National Survey of Secondary Education, U.S. Bureau of Education Bulletin 1933, no. 17, monograph no. 19. Washington, DC: U.S. Government Printing Office.

Louis, K. S. & Miles, M. B. (1990). *Improving the urban high school: What works and why*. New York: Teachers College Press.

McGrail, J. et al. (1987). *Looking at schools: Instruments and processes for school analysis*. Washington, DC: Office of Educational Research and Improvement. (ERIC Document Reproduction Service No. ED 280 885).

National Center for Education Statistics [Online]. Available: Http://nces.ed.gov [1999].

National Commission on Excellence in Education. (1983). *A nation at risk: The imperative for educational reform*. Washington, DC: U.S. Government Printing Office.

National Commission on the Reform of Secondary Education (1973). *The reform of secondary education: A report to the public and the profession*. New York: McGraw-Hill.

National Council of Teachers of English: The list of standards for the English language arts. National Council of Teachers of English and the International Reading Association [Online]. Available: Http://ncte.org/standards/thelist.html [1999]. Extracts reprinted with permission: *Standards for the English Language Arts*, by the International Reading Association and the National Council of Teachers of English, Copyright 1996 by the International Reading Association and the National Council of Teachers of English.

National Education Association (1894). *Report of the committee of ten on secondary school studies*. New York: American Book Company.

National Endowment for the Arts: NEA partnerships [Online]. Available: Http://www.arts.endow.gov/partner [1999].

National science education standards [Online]. Available: Http://books.nap.edu/html/nses [1999]. Extracts reprinted [adapted] with permission from *National Science Education Standards*. Copyright (1996) by the National Academy of Sciences. Courtesy of the National Academy Press, Washington, DC.

National standards for arts education [Online]. Available: Http://artsedge.kennedy-center.org/forms/arts1.html [1999]. Excerpts and adaptations used by permission from *National Standards for Arts Education*. Copyright 1994 by Music Educators National Conference.

NCTM: Principles and standards for school mathematics. (2000). National Council of Teachers of Mathematics [Online]. Available: http://www.nctm.org/standards [June 10, 2000].

Nelson, J. L., Palonsky, S. B., & Carlson, K. (2000). *Critical issues in education*. New York: McGraw-Hill.

Oakes, J. & Lipton, M. (1990). *Making the best of schools: A handbook for parents, teachers, and policymakers*. New Haven, CT: Yale University Press.

Ogden, E. H. & Germinario, V. (1995). *The nation's best schools: Blueprints for excellence*. Lancaster, PA.: Technomic Publishing Company, Inc.

Position statement on appropriate staffing for school library media centers. (2000). American Association of School Librarians, American Library Association [Online]. Available: Http://www.ala.org/aasl/positions/ps_schoolmedia.html [June 8, 2000].

Powell, A. G., Farrar, E., & Cohen, D. K. (1985). *The shopping mall high school: Winners and losers in the educational marketplace.* Boston: Houghton Mifflin.

Pulliam, J. & Van Patten, J. (1995). *History of education in America.* Englewood Cliffs, NJ: Prentice-Hall.

Sizer, T. R. (1984). *Horace's compromise: The dilemma of the American high school.* Boston: Houghton Mifflin.

Sizer, T. R. (1992). *Horace's school: Redesigning the American high school.* Boston: Houghton Mifflin

Sizer, T. R. (1996). *Horace's hope: What works for the American high school.* Boston: Houghton Mifflin.

Snyder, T. D. & Hoffman, C. M. (1998). *State comparisons of education statistics: 1969–70 to 1996–97.* Washington, DC: U.S. Department of Education, Office of Educational Research and Improvement, National Center for Education Statistics.

Standards and position statements. (1997). National Council for the Social Studies (NCSS) [Online]. Available: Http://www.ncss.org/standards/home.html [1999].

Standards for foreign language learning [Online]. Available: Http://www.actfl.org/htdocs/standards/standards.htm [2000]. Extracts reprinted with permission from National Standards in Foreign Language Education Project (1999). *Standards for Foreign Language Learning in the 21st Century.* Yonkers, NY: National Standards in Foreign Language Education Project.

State departments of education [Online]. Available: Http://www.asd.com/asd/edconn/tr-doe.htm [1998].

State indicators in education 1997. (1997). Washington, DC: U.S. Department of Education, Office of Educational Research and Improvement, National Center for Education Statistics.

Teddlie, C. & Stringfield, S. (1993). *Schools make a difference: Lessons learned from a 10-year study of school effects.* New York: Teachers College Press.

Trump, J. L. & Baynham, D. (1961). *Guide to better schools.* Chicago. Rand McNally.

Turnbull, H. R. & Turnbull, A. P. (1998). *Free appropriate public education: The law and children with disabilities.* Denver: Love Publishing.

Twentieth-Century Fund. (1983). *Making the grade.* New York: Twentieth-Century Fund.

Urban, W. J. & Wagoner, J. L., Jr. (2000). *American education: A history.* New York: McGraw-Hill.

Wanko, M. A. (forthcoming). *Creating safe and supportive schools: Prevention and response.* Monroe Township, NJ: Foundation of Educational Administration.

Weiss, M. J. (April 1992). America's best schools: First annual high school report card. *Redbook, 178* (6) [Online]. Available: EBSCOhost.

Weiss, M. J. (April 1994). America's best schools. *Redbook, 182* (6), 77–87.

Wilson, B. L. & Corcoran, T. B. (1988). *Successful secondary schools: Visions of excellence in American public education.* Levittown, PA: Falmer Press, Ltd.

Index

About the Authors

DOROTHY WARNER is Associate Professor-Librarian at Rider University.

WILLIAM D. GUTHRIE is Associate Professor, Undergraduate Education, Rider University.